MW01069402

ETXEBARRI

ARGINZONIZ — AXPE

*To those who are no longer here but have been by
my side, to those who are still here and at my side,
to my professional colleagues and to my customers
who, with their selfless encouragement, helped me
endure difficult moments, to those who continue
to give me their unconditional support, I give
to you all my most heartfelt thank you.*

Bittor Arginzoniz

ETXEBARRI

ARGINZONIZ — AXPE

TEXT
JUAN PABLO CARDENAL
& **JON SARABIA**

PHOTOGRAPHS
MARIANO HERRERA

GRUB STREET — LONDON

CONTENTS

I

RAFAEL GARCÍA SANTOS

In thirty years of going to the best and most avant-garde restaurants in the world every day, on very few occasions have I seen such a natural, elegant, personal, honest, generous, earnest and sublime revolution. And such a level-headed one.

The huge achievement of Bittor Arginzoniz is to have applied relevant concepts to the grill-house that came out of the culinary revolution experienced in Spain during the last decade of the 20th century, and the first decade of the current one; principles that were disseminated around the world and that changed history. In this context, he has shone a light on haute cuisine of the hearth. And he has done it with brilliant perspicacity: universalizing the farm-house. With boundless love for the landscape, traditions and his feelings, and with intelligence that is both maverick and global, he embraces ideas and even ingredients, achieving the perfect symbiosis between history and future, between passion for his land and an openness to rational and material excellence. He has never set limits to his work, nor to the delicacies he uses, nor to any inspiration he has had. And he does all of this with a message that is unmistakably Basque and unmistakably personal. This is what a contemporary grill-house looks like, and it looks like ETXEBARRI. An exaltation of principles and an exaltation of overcoming.

This intelligent, bold homespun man has made a difference. In his quest for perfection, he began by looking at the fuel he needed to use. In the end, he substituted evolution for origins; instead of charcoal he uses woods that are more aromatic and natural, using one or another depending on the ingredients to be placed over the embers: oak for fish, grapevine wood for meat and, sometimes, vine cuttings among others. This return to the past – that has entailed more work and higher costs – reveals Arginzoniz's philosophy: a pursuit of the best and what is most authentic. Infusing his delicious food with smoke and rustic simplicity. A wise decision.

By grilling ingredients that had never been near a grill before, he had to invent ingenious tools: mesh pans like sieves; others with precisely cut laser-made holes; tiny, flat fish-grilling baskets; and even a pot with a hole in the centre – like the crater of a volcano – to steam certain kinds of seafood, such as mussels, with the wood.

He devised new ideas that brim with common sense: to avoid having to cook elvers twice – in water and then in the pan – he allowed them to cook over the heat of the embers. Brilliant. To keep the flesh as juicy as possible, he removes the spines and other bones from anchovies, butterflies them and sandwiches two together, making one double anchovy from two of them. The result is perfectly pink and rosy as they are only cooked on one side, the skin side, making them more generously sized and firmer to the bite.

He has managed to magically juggle the creaminess of a risotto by directly infusing the rice with the smoke. He has also created never-before-seen versions of goose-neck barnacles, caviar and sea cucumbers, impregnating them with subtle smoky fragrances. His chicken croquettes and orange-filled fritters are not fried but grilled, much to everyone's astonishment. Yes, large, rectangular croquettes over the embers. There are no limits to what he does.

Bittor Arginzoniz has created a wealth of iconic dishes, all cooked over wood coals, that are the backbone of his work. Perhaps the most famous are his elvers, splendid and flawless; truly unique. His semi-brined anchovies are second to none, the best of their kind in the world; semi-brined to enhance their naturalness, freshness and fleshiness, which minimises the salt needed. Exactly the same could be said of his artisanal chorizo made with minced meat sourced from Joselito; seasoned with choricero peppers instead of paprika, and cured in his farmhouse, the flavour and texture are unbeatable. His cod shines pure and iridescent in its uniqueness, able to compete and even surpass the best pilpil dishes. However, it is no longer on the menu because it is impossible to find the necessary quality. These are the jokes our friend plays on us. Another outstanding dish – for the new texture afforded to this seafood – are the oysters warmed in the hearth and served on a bed of cooked seaweed; sea, more sea and only the ocean plus a hint of rurality. This can also be said of the red shrimp, the langoustines, and the unbeatable sea cucumbers – always done on the grill – and served, in spring, with baby broad beans, or with pocha beans in summer, depending on the season. Not to mention the braised baby octopuses garnished with confit onions and a brushstroke of black sauce. The teardrop peas – grown in Bittor's vegetable garden – are magnificent; they are grilled over wood coals for a minute and served with their blended pods. On the same level of magnificence are the 'smoked' hake kokotxas, here served with a velvety, delicate emulsion inspired by the traditional green sauce. The same philosophy is applied to wild mushrooms – that vary according to the season – done over the embers with aubergines or beetroot and their jus: without a doubt, haute modern cuisine combined with fire at its most elemental and hypnotic. Another successful pairing: egg yolk with creamed potato and white or black truffle…impeccable and sumptuous. St George's mushrooms are at their peak in spring and make the best scrambled eggs that are creamy and aromatic; they make the best 'crisp' for their fragility and purity, shaped with a sheet of filo pastry covered with slices of the same mushroom and toasted over the embers; the best, by far, are the St George's mushrooms sautéed in a mesh pan over the fire itself and then arranged on a plate over an asparagus stock whose fragrance is enhanced with even more of these finely chopped mushrooms; and they are even used in a bold dessert, a sumptuous ice cream, having been infused in milk that conveys myriad hints of the woods.

It is clear that there is imagination, and lots of it, in the essential nature – and given as yet another example – of the mussels steamed over wood, with carrot juice and choricero pepper dust. There is more boldness in the down-to-earth Iberico burger, or 'txistorra' as it is also called, where the protagonist is meat from acorn-fed black pigs, and is made, to be precise, with fresh cuts of pork shoulder, meat from the Secreto cut, and the front part of the loin, seasoned with choricero peppers, garlic and salt; browned on the outside but left raw in the middle, it is lightly infused with the embers and served on a bed of potatoes that are reminiscent of gnocchi. An infinite number of astonishing ideas, worthy of a culinary artist, that also include turtle doves and woodcock grilled over wood coals and served with beetroot and chestnuts.

This is the madness that emerges from nature and from naturalness. Smoked butter; canapé of Iberico pork belly; bone marrow with truffles and celery; snails cooked in straw, served with diced Iberico pork belly and arranged on a bed of Vizcaina sauce; cod tripe on a crispy base of cod skin; eel with crispy skin and its gelatinous flesh served with a pumpkin terrine and sprinkled with cayenne pepper; the chop... We have eaten the best of the best here: the best when it comes to ingredients, the best when it comes to the cooking of the food, the best when it comes to the splendour of the wood coals, and the best when it comes to creativity that is infinitely more artistic and avant-garde than that of many showmen who are on so many flashy lists of haute cuisine cooks.

The revolution extends to his desserts. I mentioned the orange-filled fritters earlier, but don't miss out on the smoked butter madeleines or the apples baked over wood coals with smoked-milk ice cream.

An admirable man and his hearth who have conquered the world by transforming the most primal and ancient way of cooking, and the reason why Bittor Arginzoniz is in the history books of Basque gastronomy and those on gastronomy. And if that is admirable, as a person he is that and more. One is the result of the other.

'He has never set limits
to his work, nor to
the delicacies he uses,
nor to any inspiration
he has had'

II

THE FIRE WHISPERER

As we were about to go to print with the Spanish edition, we still didn't have a subtitle for this book; as we couldn't find a suitable translation to *The Fire Whisperer* which was the code name for the project for the, almost, three years that we devoted to it, and we are still unable to let go of the original English version as it perfectly defines Bittor Arginzoniz. Hence the name of this chapter remains *The Fire Whisperer* in both the Spanish and English editions.

This is a book about the Etxebarri grill-house and a book about Bittor Arginzoniz, without whom it would not have been possible. What may seem to be obvious to some in the acknowledgements became repeatedly frustrating in light of the impossibility of getting Bittor to embark on a book. Devoting half an hour to a book, even if it was about his life's work, wasn't how his mind worked. Without his acceptance and without the chance of creating the content side by side with him, nothing would have made sense, at least, not for me. It is highly unlikely that I will ever have the occasion to take part in another project like this. Bittor Arginzoniz is the most genuine exception in today's modern cooking that is rushing headlong into the future. I am convinced that responsibility and commitment are linked to family values that taught us that food was sacred and that produce was religion. He has taken this to an extreme with the formula of a farmhouse as his vehicle: the power house; however, he is the real power house. Those of us who have had the honour of spending time with him realised this in just one day and because of that we are all the more in awe of him. The fact that this phenomenon takes place in an idyllic valley at the foot of a mythological mountain has only made the legend about him grow, almost as if he were a yeti or a *basajaun* [an enormous, hirsute hominid who lives in the woods]. But, maybe, what most pleases me about this man is that Bittor enjoys eating, and his cuisine is totally consistent and coherent with his principles.

With a small kitchen team and few front-of-house staff, to handle reservations, with no PR agent, let alone being on social networks, Bittor Arginzoniz's Etxebarri has managed to become one of the best restaurants in the world and, without a shadow of a doubt, the most atypical in its class. Of course, this is because of his ascent up the lists, but, above all due to esteem from customers, gastronomes and – I'd be willing to bet – chefs themselves, many of them foreign, who have made the pilgrimage to Axpe and underwent an epiphany. Something of a virgin on the gastronomic media scene, which acclaims him but does not stop him from cooking every day, his appearance on the late Anthony Bourdain's show did much to catapult Etxebarri to becoming a restaurant destination; you could say that Bourdain turned him into a celebrity, as he cheerily declared it to be the place he'd like to die while eating. It also helped that Michael Pollan devoted a chapter to him in his best-selling book *Cooked,* precisely to illustrate the possibilities of cooking over fire in the 21st century and its reinvention thanks to Bittor.

That said, some of us knew that what was going on in Axpe was of galactic dimensions and we foresaw the phenomenon that was going to be unleashed – much to Bittor's dismay – because we are unaware of any restaurant of such ranking where the chef does not delegate the buying of produce and the execution of dishes; at least, not in the league of Michelin-starred restaurants nor those among The World's 50 Best Restaurants. It is, of course, noteworthy and also comforting to see him go from 34 to 13, then to 10 then 6, and in the latest edition, to 10. All in a very short space of time, and in such a way that, above all, over the past three years, he has attracted many people curious about him, as well as gastronomic tourists. There are probably those who can't understand the fuss, but the truth is that the food now at Etxebarri is better than ever, and in line with his media success.

Without wanting to justify anything, this book aims to share what we experienced with Bittor and tells the tale of Etxebarri in a somewhat systematic way. Bittor, his habitat (Axpe), the story of Etxebarri and the core elements of its cuisine: produce, fire and the extraordinarily painstaking work done in the kitchen. As it is, from the inside. I sometimes thought that we could have survived without a book about Etxebarri, and just left it as a place of pilgrimage. Too late.

But it is good to highlight the concepts, at least the most basic, the most irrefutable. I vividly recall my first visit to Axpe almost two decades ago, enticed by the writings of the great Rafa García Santos, its discovery and that of many other things. For a local Basque guy, the landscape and the format were not surprising, except for the feeling that I was approaching a temple of cuisine based on seasonal produce with the most awards of the day, and the added curiosity of seeing his innovations regarding the grill. On successive visits the excitement has remained and the path to Axpe has become one of revelations.

During that first meal, extraordinary things began to happen. When a cook surprises you with a particular dish it is what you expect when you go there on purpose, but when it happens with every single dish, it moves you. In quick succession, Bittor Arginzoniz presented a series of dishes that did not look like examples of haute cuisine and that, emotionally, moved me. Chorizo, butter, lobster, prawns, cockles, turbot, elvers (Bilbao style), elvers (grilled), chop, ice cream. One of those days when Bittor was at his very best. I had been lucky enough to have had a general education in gastronomy with access to this produce at home and in the best restaurants, but it seemed to me that this guy was interpreting each food in the best way I had ever seen and, perhaps, would ever see. With fire and a grill, over wood coals. Obviously, with the aroma of smoke, or cooked over the fire without smoking, creating a poignant feeling of returning to the essence of things, to the purity of cooking and flavours at their most impressive. Cooking time and temperature. Legendary.

Let's go back in time to October 2014, when I finally managed – after various calls – to sit down at the bar with Bittor on the ground floor of the restaurant where, over the following months, we would talk for hours and hours. For some reason, he agreed to be the protagonist of this book, after working for 25 years, and which he has no doubt regretted. And so, he put himself in the hands of someone with almost no credentials other than being a customer. But he set two conditions: one, I don't want to make anything from this; two, I don't want it to cost me anything. By cost he was not referring to money, but to disrupting the day-to-day work in the kitchen and the experience of his customers. That's how it happened and that's how this book was created, with honesty and respect. And with intervals, much to the despair of my publishing partner. Even with these conditions and with few resources, I didn't hesitate to leap into producing what is now a reality. I knew that patience would be needed with Bittor, not because it would run out, but because of the need to observe and wait for the content to emerge. Basically – and said in hindsight after a few adventures – it had to be done using a team that was discreet and completely trustworthy. Not much of a script was necessary.

Etxebarri gave me the chance to enjoy sharing the kinds of meals that Juan Pablo Cardenal also likes. He has been a cornerstone of this documentary journey, used to researching before setting off on a trip, and differentiating the story of a book from its rhythm. Without respecting Bittor's time and priorities, and without that empathy, we weren't going to achieve a lot. Bittor doesn't talk much, and talks even less when he is asked something. There wasn't even a folder of menus or recipes (what for?), and he asked, 'What recipe do you need for elvers that are sautéed in a spoonful of oil over wood coals for just a few seconds in a homemade sieve?' Beyond the story, our aim is to convey Bittor's way of working, the key ways he chooses produce and the way he treats it. But there's more: tiny differentiating details that reveal that at Etxebarri there's more cooking going on than what is apparent, the result of which would be impossible without Bittor's own hardware designs or the finishing touches done by his team: all done so that when the moment arrives, the grill chef can unravel the mystery of each item he grills to perfection, every day and for every dish, at the helm of his ship.

Inquisitive diners approach the grills for a few minutes, it's hellish. An entire service is diabolical to do, but years and years offering the same results can only be achieved by the greatest, whatever the job. Someone who best knows the kitchen at Etxebarri – and is not a cook – is Mariano Herrera, the photographer. Mariano, who immediately understood the calibre of his subject, enthusiastically joined the project yet remained at a discreet distance to shadow Bittor to instantly achieve the most faithful results. Up close and from afar, at home and atop the Anboto. Capturing what goes on in a kitchen as it happens is no easy feat: the lighting was poor and everything was done live, in the heat of the moment. No styling, no repetitions, no planned shoots when service was over; that's how it is there and that's how we decided to do it. The photographs in this book are the only ones possible to take, but we are delighted as they are exactly what we were looking for – a broader perspective; and the same thing happened with the text. Due to our different backgrounds we used other lenses – our own – but we were given the chance to do so and here is the result.

Jon Sarabia, Axpe, June 2017

'This book is, above all,
a story and the culinary notes
of a place and a unique
person: *The Fire Whisperer*'

1

Looking towards the peak, Bittor Arginzoniz adjusts his boots and sets off. He is heading to one of the crests of the Urkiola Nature Reserve, along a path whose terrain is steep and rocky. The ascent is demanding and the narrow, uneven path fades as it steepens, forcing the path to cut a zigzag into the mountainside. Bittor sets himself a good uphill pace so that he can do the twenty-two-kilometre loop that winds through this natural landscape he has known since childhood in less than four hours. Depending on the season, he crosses snow-capped peaks, walks through damp meadows suffused with green, or follows steep paths that penetrate deciduous woods carpeted with fallen leaves.

This tradition – that Bittor has fulfilled alone every Monday for twenty-five years – would be demanding for any mere mortal, but for him it is, above all, a release, a moment of calm, an act of redemption in itself. The physical exertion serves to let off steam and helps him stay in shape; it is a counterbalance to the relentless pace at Etxebarri that demands his total devotion the other six days of the week. 'Being a cook means you have to be in shape both physically as well as mentally, just like a top sportsperson. If you aren't, you haven't got much hope: you can't work well, you become disinterested and lose all your creativity,' he says with conviction.

Trapped daily by routines and blind to everything but what is immediate, his Monday hikes have a soothing effect. Being alone in nature allows Bittor to change his pace, take a step back and think clearly; it inspires new ideas in him as well as ways to improve what he offers on his menu. It is also a reencounter with his past. Almost at the top, the shrine of Saint Barbara is an essential halt. For decades it was a place of pilgrimage for the locals of Axpe during Holy Week. Bittor recalls that, as a child, they would walk for hours up the mountain in single file. The strongest among them would carry a great cross on their backs all the way to the shrine where the village priest celebrated mass.

From a thousand metres above sea level, the view of the Atxondo Valley is nothing short of majestic. The spurs of the Urkiola mountains rise up, home to the hidden cave which gave rise to the legend of the witch of the Anboto. From afar, the rustic buildings of Axpe, including the Asador Etxebarri, appear wrapped in mint-green meadows. Cows, sheep and horses graze in them, under the watchful eyes of the sheepdogs. The entire valley is dotted with old farmhouses, curls of smoke drifting from their chimneys. High up, you can see the clouds of smoke merge with the mist or the snow, or just making their way upwards through the rain and the blue sky. Only the wind cleaves the silence.

With its exuberant nature, its traditions and its unassertive way of life, this remote place in the Basque Country has an existential meaning for Bittor. This habitat converges with his bond with the land, with his family's roots, and with the space in which collective history has been forged over generations. A memory that has survived until now thanks to successive daily acts of heroism that shaped a way of life and a way of being. The surroundings where Bittor grew up together with his loved ones is at the heart of this unconditional affection he has for his own land: Atxondo is his home in the most deeply-felt sense of the word, his emotional refuge, the spinal column of his life. Loyalty to his origins and his devotion to nature have firmly anchored him there.

So, it is hardly surprising that this micro cosmos in the Basque Country that imbues his life with meaning has been etched into his genes in blood and fire. He has spent his entire life there: born in Axpe in 1960, he grew up in a local farmhouse called Olazábal immersed in the hardships of the rural life of those days but, when he had the chance to leave, he decided to stay. Both Etxebarri, inaugurated in 1990, and the family farmhouse where he lives, are within a radius of less than a kilometre of each other. All these rural surroundings, Basque ways and customs, his attachment to nature, the values instilled in him, and his fierce belief in the family cause are factors that, throughout his life, have seeped, like a fine drizzle, into Bittor's personality. They culminated in the creation of a second skin that he has never wanted to shake off.

The important result of all of this is that Etxebarri could not have existed in any other place in the world. His culinary project would have been a business or, literally, just a way to earn a living. But what is more important in Bittor's view is that Etxebarri is, above all else, a philosophy of life. So, the fact that it is located in Axpe is not fortuitous: it is bound to Bittor's commitment to his past, to his wish to live by values that are sacred for him and, what is more, to do it in surroundings that he has chosen. He did not betray his roots when his culinary prowess became recognised, and opportunities – even tempting ones – came knocking at his door.

New challenges, horizons to discover, the opening of new restaurants, offers to link his name to eateries in far-off places. For Bittor it was a no-brainer: he rejected every one. Not even the idea of setting foot in Bilbao and leaving his mark on the city that had always been in his emotional orbit – and is only 43 kilometres from his place of birth – had enough power to seduce and convince him. It is truly difficult to imagine what might push Bittor to forsake the principles he believes in. It is certainly not money. In fact, as can be deduced from the soundness of what he offers on his menu, what sets Bittor apart from many other colleagues in his profession is that he has never wanted to be a businessman. His way is, simply, a life devoted to a passion. And his passion is cooking.

Achieving this goal so successfully and having made Axpe the epicentre of his life is an extraordinary feat, although an act such as this does not always arouse the attention it deserves. It isn't simply that Bittor didn't have the educational possibilities that would have endowed him with invaluable baggage. It is that, in those circumstances, he was able to go off-script in surroundings as closed and rural as those of Axpe, where standing out is much harder than in more dynamic places. This shows what he is made of, because overcoming nothingness in the midst of perpetual routine is something only the best of the best can achieve. His singular talent and personality certainly account for the scale of his achievement: making Etxebarri – located in this remote corner of the Basque Country – one of the best restaurants in the world.

How did he make such a miracle happen? The above-mentioned geographical and family contexts, of course, were hugely influential. Bittor was brought up in a family which, despite its modest economic means, made meals a daily discovery. The stew that his mother and grandmother made every day, and cooked over wood coals in the family farmhouse, came about thanks to a very close relationship they both had with food. The almost mystical respect they had in his home for produce – is now, it would appear, one of the current hallmarks of Basque gastronomic culture – was unwittingly assimilated by Bittor in his culinary designs for Etxebarri. As at every traditional grill-house, the cooking was simple, but the quality of the produce was indisputable.

Over the years, Bittor took this philosophy to new heights. Just as it was in many other grill-houses, Etxebarri's menu was quite basic to begin with. It was cooking that used local ingredients, in other words, it was based on locally-sourced raw materials that were char-grilled or griddled and which, when served up, were garnished with the usual fried garlic. However, when it came to the fire and the wood coals, these were what fuelled the gastronomic revolution of the restaurant, and Bittor's usual passion for choosing authentic, quality raw materials became an obsession. He was dead right about one thing: he discovered the magic of fire; rather than transforming foods into something different, it contributed to showing them as they really are.

It became, therefore, imperative to use first-rate ingredients from the moment it was clear that the technical skill involved in managing the wood coals enhanced their attributes and natural qualities. Etxebarri thus entered another dimension: reborn were the aromas of nature, of the family farmhouse, of the stew that bubbled away for hours at a simmer. Furthermore, native produce and seasonality became even more relevant because since then, and until today, what is essential for Bittor is that the raw materials reveal their true, authentic flavours. But it's not just that: it is also important for the produce to make sense for him on an emotional level. If he can't connect with it, he won't use it. 'Why is this important for me? How do I explain it?' he asks himself every time he has to weigh up whether or not to put a new item on the menu.

This new dawn in grilling brought about a change in concept the great contribution of which resulted in a distinct, even impressive, shift in cooking, yet still respected traditional flavours and remained faithful to them. In this attraction that Bittor feels for produce, a sensitivity – almost Japanese, if you like – can be felt, and which, without a doubt, begins with the search and selection of the best raw materials, continues with flawless knife skills, respectful treatment, and culminates in beautiful presentation. What seems so obvious is not, in fact, at all easy to achieve: the filter of sophistication and quality that Bittor applies to what he offers conflicts with the facts because being supplied with the best produce is an increasingly difficult mission.

Achieving the quality he demands requires formidable dedication and effort. In the first place, he transformed his farmhouse into a sort of power-house

CONTINUES »

'Being a cook means you have to be in shape both physically as well as mentally, just like a top sportsperson. If you aren't, you haven't got much hope: you can't work well, you become disinterested and lose all your creativity'

of gastronomic craftsmanship. There he produces, grows, dries and breeds everything he can: from buffaloes, chickens and beer, to fruit trees, herbs and vegetables during every season of the year. This means that at Etxebarri, local seasonal vegetables – picked when they are their very best – are enjoyed all year round. That is not the only example: mozzarella is made daily with buffalo milk, milked that very morning; the scrambled eggs are made with eggs gathered that day; and the stock is made with chickens and hens fed on corn and slaughtered just hours before going into the pot.

What Bittor cannot produce himself he searches for, needless to say, at the market. This task to seek produce is an absolute quest. Of course, with just a phone call anyone can have a crate of seafood, meat or vegetables delivered right to the kitchen table every morning. No doubt this is a more direct way of getting supplies and one, furthermore, that requires much less dedication, but the drawback is that the quality of the produce becomes much more touch and go. In fact, even if the raw materials measure up, it is never enough for Bittor. What he has been doing for over two decades is not a search for good produce, but a thorough exploration until he finds the best. He only gives his approval when the produce is perfect.

This level of excellence is achieved almost exclusively thanks to systematic dedication that is respected daily. Bittor spent half of his life going, in person, to the fish markets along the Cantabrian coast so that it would be him, and not someone else, choosing the fish. He went all over Spain to find the right supplier to provide him with the beef that had the properties he required. He researched endlessly to discover a herdsman who could sell him sheep's milk every week; to find the best quality Mediterranean red shrimp; or for the Iberico pork he uses for his artisanal chorizo to have been recently slaughtered and delivered to Etxebarri via the perfect cold chain. The difficulty lies in the little window that spans the good to the unbeatable, but it is a challenge that Bittor has always faced unwaveringly.

It is true that as soon as he established a relationship of trust with his suppliers, some of the pressure was lifted. But it is also true that the time saved is invested in new challenges. For instance, the solution he came up with to avoid having to cook elvers twice led him to set up an aquarium to keep them alive. The sophistication of the technical skill in managing the wood coals required his all, beginning with the construction of wood-fired ovens set apart from the kitchen. At the same time, introducing new foods to be cooked over fire requires much trial and error before coming up with the perfect cooking process. And the desire to make craft beer at his farmhouse, despite his initial inexperience, is just another example of the extraordinary magic that he imbues into everything he creates.

This touch of seduction and perfection that infuses his cuisine and makes it shine emanates from his irresistible personality: that of a man who is convinced of what he is doing, and that of a cook who is happy in his habitat. He begins his day as the sun rises and goes for a ten-kilometre run in the woods, his source of inspiration. His daily routines until service are the embodiment of vitality, a combination of talent and logistics: suppliers, choosing the produce, making the dishes of the day, checking and testing various things. As soon as the first diners arrive, nothing will make him budge from the grill where, like an artist of fire, he reveals his skills with the concentration of a chess player. During this time he never enters the dining room, ever: 'I mingle with diners when service is over, never before. That is sacred,' he declares. Bittor has internalised the fact that in his profession he must always be there because excellence is almost always in the detail.

His extraordinary threshold for sacrifice is, needless to say, a vital ingredient in his recipe for success. But where the effort ends and his perfectionism begins is a line that is much harder to distinguish. The knowledge gleaned from both have helped to forge a man who is supremely self-demanding, disciplined and indefatigable in reaching his goals, in addition to being a human being with a special sensitivity to give his creations a remarkable touch of magic. All these attributes serve as a stimulus and are at the core of what is his extreme gastronomy. The impact on the final result is impossible to disregard. Bittor is not guided by effort for his dishes to be impeccable. He gives it his all when he cooks. As his wish is to offer perfection, there is love in every dish. And if the resulting dish is not perfect, it doesn't reach the table.

To truly appreciate the fact that Bittor is recognised as the creator of haute-cuisine grilling we must, naturally, look at his humble origins and the setting in which he was raised. But what is absolutely heroic is that Bittor has been able to write such a beautiful gastronomic story without ever having had formal culinary training, nor worked in any other kitchen, nor stayed in touch with other cooks. Generally speaking, one would say that Bittor is self-taught and, thanks to a great combination of tenacity, intuition, sensitivity and boldness, he discovered – little by little – what has now become a culinary rule-book, despite the fact that when he started out, everything was new to him. Opening up an unexplored path without the direction and guidance of instruction is a miracle conferred on the exceptionally gifted.

Bittor's journey has, without a doubt, been marked by everything that he imbued at home throughout his life. The food critic – and gastronomic father – Rafael García Santos, later played a decisive role by helping to anchor, perfect and develop the menu at Etxebarri just when it was at a turning point.

But, paradoxically, and not taking other people into account, what had a massive influence on Bittor's menu was that he was not able to offer a more refined and creative cuisine simply because nobody had taught it to him. This pushed him towards a simpler kind of cooking – like the one he saw his mother and grand-mother prepare – that was based on fire. In the years that followed, once he had set his course, he took this kind of cooking to the highest level of refinement.

This isolation took him along his own roads and resulted in very personal signature dishes, free from external influences. Bittor, indeed, recognises that his ways of doing things and his commitment make it hard for him to leave Axpe, although out of intellectual curiosity and because the knowledge of others is a logical source of inspiration, he tries to stay abreast of trends in other places. He has, however, applied concepts and techniques of haute cuisine to what he offers at the grill-house but, in a way, his circumstances and his personality have shielded him from bad foreign habits, in particular during the splendid years of haute cuisine when, if you didn't create anything, you were a nobody. Going against the flow and distancing himself from ideas that were repeated and were evolved ad nauseam have endowed his gastronomic project with harmony.

His is, therefore, a singular and honest cuisine. A cuisine of earth, sea and fire. Elemental and delicate. A culinary art without shortcuts, based on a simple concept centred on produce which, in itself, is a remarkable challenge because the simplest things are usually the most difficult. Yet, at the same time, the level of complexity and sophistication involved in his cooking has an irresistible power of seduction. Fire – of course! – plays a decisive role, and Bittor has mastered it thanks to an arduous lesson of trial and error. At Etxebarri he unleashes his exultant control over the flames: the magic of technically perfect grilling over wood coals, and smoke as the sixth basic taste that gives flavour to all his crea-tions. With this signature style, Bittor has accomplished an emphatic achievement: to give a qualitative leap to the concept of the grill-house.

He has brought about this revolution by cooking from his soul and with his heart. 'It all comes from within me, I know what I like and I act on that. This is my journey, the one I think I should follow because it is the one I like and the one I believe in. If, when you do something, you don't feel it; why would you dedicate yourself to it?'. His goal, as he often points out, is to satisfy people and make them happy. He owes it to his customers: he loves cooking, and relishes conveying to the table the pleasure he feels when cooking for the enjoyment of his diners. The sacrifice it entails requires paying a huge toll, 'but there is more to it than money, and that is that people feel happy here,' he declares.

What Bittor offers on his menu is, thus, nothing less that an unalloyed extension of his way of life. His personality infuses his cuisine, he is his culinary offering. Bittor is, perhaps, a prisoner of his work, but he never sought fame or riches. Money is the passion of others, his is cooking. Bittor is an example of Basque elegance and identity. He is, in short, an unassuming, honest and idealistic person who wanted to be someone in the world of cooking and has achieved it. He is nothing more than a cook who is happy doing what he does.

2

Axpe is the ultimate haven of tranquillity. A mountainous, bucolic, remote spot. Where life is solitary and the pace is slow. Thoroughly Basque. Almost unpeopled, there are barely 200 inhabitants scattered over dozens of farms. Devoted to their roots, traditions and charters (known as *fueros*). A fertile hotbed of mythology. A place where bells peal each liturgical hour. Rural and livestock-raising par excellence. Witness to harsh winters, heavy skies and greyish light. Of rain-soaked secondary roads. Of mist that glides down the hillsides. A place where the wind slices and the earth smells damp. An unchanging paradise in the heart of the Basque Country. In the far south east of the province of Biscay, it makes up the little district of the Valley of Atxondo, a municipality it shares with the ancient *elizates* of Apatamonasterio and Arrazola since they were merged in 1962. The valley opens up to the north towards the River Ibaizábal, fed by a network of small streams. In the south east, it is cut off, almost violently, by the peaks of the Anboto Sierra that form an enormous mountain barrier that defends, on the border with Álava, the entire province of Duranguesado. The karstic hulk of the Anboto, that rises 1,296 metres above sea level, presides over the Urkiola Nature Reserve.

The precipitation that falls on the north face of this unique reserve courses to the Cantabrian Sea, while that on the other side flows to the River Ebro. The limestone sides of its crags are, in fact, a consequence of water erosion; this has also resulted in a perforated subsoil where many caves – some unexplored – can be found. In one of them, situated just below the peak on the vertical wall of the east face of the Anboto, and often shrouded in mist, lives 'the Mari', a witch of the coven and goddess of pre-Christian mythology, worshipped by the local shepherds. A divinity who, over the centuries, has become a popular legend fuelled by the thirst of people who seek explanations for everything that surrounds them and, above all, what they fear.

Long ago, mythological beings corresponded to an elemental perception of good and bad. 'The Mari' holds sway over the forces of nature and, therefore, is responsible for the wind and lightning, as well as storms and hailstorms and she punishes those who lie, steal, are arrogant or do not keep their word. She has a female's face and body, like a woman of fire, like a hybrid of a tree and a woman with the legs of a goat and the claws of a bird of prey. According to folklore, she has also been seen in the guise of a goat and of a horse. The late Christianisation of the most remote and off-the-beaten-track parts of the Basque lands explains the continued belief in superstitions that went well into the Middle Ages.

Christianisation entered precisely through the Urkiola mountain range, leaving in its wake a rosary of shrines and churches. The pronounced slopes of the peaks of this nature reserve, down to the valley where the River Ibaizábal snakes its way, is littered with reasons why this land was depopulated over the course of history. It also draws a rugged landscape where beech groves and other native woods, reforested areas, idyllic meadows and steep, dangerous paths coexist and are interwoven. The great variety of habitats, with woods of beech, holm oak and oak trees, create environments that are almost always damp, making it an extraordinarily micological environment.

This unique ecosystem – only thirty kilometres from the sea – coalesces a series of excellent meteorological conditions. It is an area with much rain, dampness and mist, but not particularly cold or excessively hot. The Anboto and other crags of the Urkiola range protect, to some extent, the effects of the south wind, the worst enemy that wild mushrooms have. Orographically speaking, the half dozen peaks that make up the crags of the Duranguesado are a wonderful habitat for St George's mushrooms, a local gem. When it is cold, they sprout on the slopes at about 400 metres above sea level; when it gets hot, they are gathered close to the peaks, at over 1,000 metres. At this altitude, St George's mushrooms release their aroma.

Other wild mushrooms such as porcini, March mushrooms and horn of plenty mushrooms, among others, need a wooded environment like that of the Olaeta hills which, at 700 metres above sea level, separate the provinces of Álava and Biscay. This combination of climatic, geographic and orographic characteristics converge in the area – in a radius of 40 kilometres – that surrounds the restaurant Etxebarri. The micological abundance that grows around here is a gift from nature: the authentic flavours of what is local converges with the freshness of being so close, and the magic of seasonality.

These woods are also where migratory birds winter in the north of the Iberian Peninsula, seeking refuge in this ideal habitat for part of the year. The jewel among them is the woodcock that, during the cold central-European winters, enjoys the milder climate there. The exodus of the queen of the woods, probably one of the most enigmatic birds to frequent our habitats, is the drive behind a dynamic hunting season. Lasting barely three months, it attracts huge numbers of hunters to an area that has a deep-rooted tradition of hunting. Both of these – wild mushrooms and woodcocks – leave a distinctive mark on the local gastronomy and on that of Etxebarri, too.

Flocks of Latxa sheep – the iconic and native breed of the Basque Country – also graze in these surroundings and, because of their agility and untamed character, have adapted perfectly to the craggy land and to the generous rainfall of the Urkiola. They share their habitat with – also native – Pottok horses; a semi-feral breed of pony that is very hardy and strong, and at home in mountainous terrain. Since time immemorial they have been faithful allies to the people of this rural area: They have been used for hunting, for ploughing and as draught horses on farms to drag tree trunks from the woods and, not so long ago, to pull carts loaded with minerals from the old local mines.

Copper, lead, tin, iron and other minerals were mined there for centuries and, in his day, an arms factory was even set up in Atxondo to provide weapons for Philip II's troops. Sites, many of them with women's names – la Profunda, la Caprichosa, la Violeta, la Preciosa – that, years later, attracted immigration and development and, at the peak of their activity, brought the miracle of the railway all the way to Atxondo. Inaugurated in 1904, the Durango-Elorrio railway line traversed the valley for 11 kilometres, stopping in Apatamonasterio from where the branch line went to Arrazola and the halt that was close to the mines.

Atxondo paid a high price. Decades of constant mining activity mutilated the landscape and poisoned the springs, disrupting the peace and the valley's traditional way of life. From the 1920s onwards, and due to their low profitability, the mines were gradually shut down. The mine trains were headed for an inevitable decline that took time to come to an end, but that also helped – before closing for good in the 1950s – as it was a means of transport for travellers and for the timber industry. When the mining came to a stop, Atxondo returned to a state of lethargy and became silent once again. Those old railway lines are today delightful green pathways.

Yet, halfway along, between the Biscay coast and the plateau of Castile, the very industrial region of Duranguesado rises up. Despite its geographic closeness and the fact that Atxondo is one of the thirteen municipal districts, they are opposite, and almost incompatible, worlds. All of a sudden, the productive pulse of the district begins to ebb as the imposing scenery of the Anboto announces, curve by curve, the approach to Axpe. Time has stopped in the square of the rural Gothic-Renaissance-style church of St John the Baptist, built in 1552. Between the river and the peaks, life flows in slow motion. One hears the occasional bark of a dog, the splashing of the fountain, the thump of a ball from the municipal *frontón* court, and perhaps a polite greeting in Euskera, borne by the wind.

They accompany the former town hall (now a gastronomic association), the school that Bittor attended, the shrine of St Ángel de la Guarda, and the pub that is today the splendid restaurant Etxebarri. Ochre roofs, ancient stone buildings, wind, stillness and mystery. The life of the community, then more than today, was centred around it. Historically, Axpe and eleven other Biscay *elizates* belonged to the *merindad* or country subdivision of Durango, a jurisdiction set up to deal with common problems – from farming and the use of woodland, to setting the boundaries of land – of the isolated districts and farms that were part of the same parish.

It enjoyed a certain amount of autonomy from the governmental bodies of the Lordship of Biscay, and had its own charter *(fuero)* that was different from the towns where artisans and tradesmen lived, in houses that made up streets that were, in turn, protected by a town wall. If the *elizates* governed communal life and the *merindades* that of a group of them, the farmhouse was, back then, the bastion of family life. Their forerunners were wooden huts that workers and shepherds erected on the sunny slopes along the River Ibaizábal's course, before being constructed of wood and stone. In Duranguesado today, there are still a thousand of the 40,000 old farmhouses that survive in the Basque Country.

These rural dwellings were built on farming and livestock holdings of 45 hectares that were worked by the family clan. Large buildings that were architecturally sound, they were home to people and animals alike: the kitchen, large hallway and other rooms were at the front of the house, and the stables, hayloft and attic were at the back. Working the land (wheat, apples, corn) and animal

CONTINUES »

'Eating is honesty and respect as part of humility. That's what I was taught at home'

husbandry (cattle, sheep, chickens, pigs) were the main activities, and were both consumed as well as sold. Over time, traditional crops were abandoned and production focused on urban demand, thus bringing about a rise in market gardens.

This rural environment, where home and family were an indivisible institution, was where Bittor spent his childhood. Over the past decades, the gradual loss of this way of life has, little by little, diluted the landscape and the cultural context that had shaped the ways of rural Basque people for centuries. Bittor has, however, somehow managed to keep it alive, not only by making his own farm and farmhouse the epicentre of his life, as in the days of old, but because he uses it not only as a dwelling. The Arginzoniz family farm is, in fact, quite the opposite; it is a 21st-century power house devoted to agriculture and livestock that embodies echoes of the past. While this ancestral way of life that is anchored to one's roots and to nature is waning all over the Basque Country, Bittor has adapted it to our times.

Thanks to that, he lives in the place he has chosen. Surrounded by nature – something that is non-negotiable for him – he cultivates the land and raises animals in the same environment where past generations did exactly the same. Just as it has always been, Bittor's existence revolves around the farm and the activities carried out there. Land that, despite its slopes, is productive every season of the year. Buffaloes are milked each morning and chickens lay eggs every day. Production that is extraordinary in our day and age. Local, seasonal, authentic, flavour. All with one destination: Etxebarri, the restaurant. No middle men, no logistics, no refrigeration. From the fields and the farm, straight to the kitchen table.

Of the domestic animals, his buffaloes – the successors of the cows of old – deserve special mention. If, in the past, cattle were raised to be sold for both meat and milk, buffaloes today are used exclusively for the production of milk. For Bittor, it is the best and, of all farm animals, has the least fat, hence he didn't mind making the long journey to the outskirts of Rome to buy a pair of buffaloes and transport them back to Axpe. He now has seven of them, five of which are females and give between 12 and 15 litres of milk a day.

With this production, he makes both fresh cheese and mozzarella on a daily basis. As a youngster, Bittor had learned how to make cheese and junket at home, but to make fresh cheese and mozzarella he had to familiarise himself with other timings and temperatures needed. But aside from the fact that they are on the menu every day at Etxebarri and that they have won gastronomic awards, these fresh cheeses are important to Bittor for another reason. Dairy products in general, and cheese in particular, have always been part of people's diet in the Basque Country, especially for those living on farms. A tradition that is even more deeply rooted, if that is possible, in Atxondo, and is why it is almost a duty for Bittor – perhaps an unwitting one – for cheese to be such a part of Etxebarri.

The buffaloes are free to roam and graze in the meadow next to the farmhouse. Octavio is the herdsman who takes care of them. He cleans out the shed every day. He feeds the bulls with alfalfa and hay, and the females with fodder, corn, cereals and hay. In summer, he hoses them down. He is there when they give birth. He washes the females' udders with hot water and milks them every morning, and separates the calves from their mothers. A huge daily effort that results in a unique fresh cheese that is ready barely 20 hours after the animals have been milked. For Bittor it is worth it.

The family farm is also home to hens, chickens and roosters, about 200 in total, that also freely come and go from the chicken coop as they please. Octavio gathers between 40 and 50 eggs each day, a fairly small number, bearing in mind the number of laying birds. This is a consequence of the natural diet – based on corn, barley and wild plants – they are given. 'As they don't eat commercial feed, they lay fewer eggs,' Octavio points out. Three geese live in the chicken coop as well; their job is to scare off the foxes that prowl around the farm as this stresses the hens and they stop laying. The geese are the guards of the farm and their honking frightens the foxes, making them flee.

Old hens that no longer lay are slaughtered almost every day, as are chickens, and both go into Etxebarri's extraordinary stock. It is the last vestige of the tradition of slaughtering animals to be eaten at the farmhouse; in general, it was pigs that were the great staple of the family. Only the making of chorizo – done in a very similar way to that which Bittor used to see years ago – remains of the traditional slaughter, as the elegant meat of the Iberico pig he uses is now supplied from Extremadura and not from pigs raised on the farm. On the other hand, choricero peppers grow in Bittor's vegetable garden; grown and dried following age-old methods.

Bittor's vegetable garden is a true gem. In addition to being totally organic, it is a wonder of tradition, local production and authentic flavours: no insecticides, fertiliser or chemical products are used. When the land is exhausted it is given natural fertiliser, either wood ash or manure, preferably from sheep. The harsh winters means growing hardy vegetables that can withstand the cold, and even the snow: leeks, carrots, beetroots, parsley, celery, swiss chard, collard greens and other members of the cabbage family, etc. During these months, a greenhouse is used where myriad herbs and flowers, as well as lettuces are grown, and is one of the restaurant's best-kept secrets.

Not only are vegetables and greens not grown in it – because plastic affects their flavour, especially that of tomatoes – but in spring and summer the plastic is removed and everything is grown in the open air. Red and white onions in March, peppers and potatoes in April, tomatoes in May. Followed by pumpkins, broad beans, peas, garlic, courgettes and artichokes among others. Everything requires tremendous dedication: ploughing the earth with the tractor; preparing the ground with organic fertiliser; making the furrows by hand; planting; watering when it doesn't rain; and weeding with a hoe...work carried out every day and plant by plant. Then, each morning and depending on what is needed at Etxebarri, produce is picked. Only what is going to be eaten is taken; otherwise, it is better left in the ground.

Such is Bittor's devotion to authenticity and the naturalness of what we eat there, that he now makes his own craft beer. The Basque Country has no beer-making tradition, although it does produce cider and Txakoli wine, two drinks typical of the region. Bittor had never made it before either, but the desire to broaden the range of beers on offer at Etxebarri was greater than his inexperience, 'If I get something into my head, I don't stop until I achieve it.' And so, in 2013, he fitted out and prepared a space in the farmhouse where he set up the equipment and quickly learned the technique and how to make it.

He wasn't very happy with the first batch, but he gradually improved its nuances until he had a good, yet refreshing, beer that also had a great balance between body, acidity and flavour. The spring water that flows straight from the mountains and also supplies the restaurant is, due to its quality, the most important factor in the production process. Everything else is a question of time and temperature.

3

Bittor's childhood in the family farmhouse was imbued with the aromas of the daily stew mingled with the smoke of wood coals. These permeating perfumes, the perfect expression of a rural life entwined with nature, could be inhaled first thing in the morning when his mother and grandmother – Narcisa and Eugenia – lay the wood for the fire, setting over it the pot where the lunchtime stew would simmer away. Back then, these farmhouses didn't have electricity so firewood was the only source of heat, both for staving off the cold and for cooking. Narcisa and Eugenia's culinary devotion, homemade food and fire made up Bittor's everyday landscape during those years.

There were always vegetables and pulses in the pot. Leeks, collard greens and peas, among many others, all homegrown. Pork was also common, and a food eaten by the family all year long. Very rarely did they treat themselves to kid or veal, in those days delicacies that were practically inaccessible. Fish, with the occasional exception of salt cod, was almost unheard of. The sea is fairly close to Axpe, but the geographical barrier was insurmountable because nobody owned a vehicle. 'I used to go to Durango with my father to sell vegetables in the square. It's just 10 kilometres away, but as we went in a donkey-drawn cart, we were away all day,' Bittor recalls.

Life on the farm was very demanding. The Arginzoniz family, like most of the people who at that time lived in rural parts of the Basque Country, dedicated themselves to agriculture and livestock. Cows, sheep, pigs and other animals were raised for their own consumption and to be sold as well, but they required total devotion. 'You had to be very careful and watch over them all the time,' Bittor reminisces. He would get up at five in the morning to milk the cows, then go to school, only to hurry back home because he had to help his father with whatever he was doing. Depending on the day, he would take care of the cows, gather firewood in the hills or work in the vegetable garden. 'I don't remember having had a childhood. There was a lot of work to do,' he explains.

This austere way of life that revolved around animals had a profound effect on Bittor. His existence and his way of being remained anchored forever in the family farmhouse and the nature that surrounds it. That life in common, shared by three generations pulling together, also forged a very tight family bond. That close relationship was sealed by Bittor's grandmother and mother's culinary stamp who, with their devotion to that modest pot of food, made meals a daily event. Mealtimes were, therefore, sacred: only when the whole family was seated around the table was the pot placed in the centre and the food served. Lunchtime was both a gastronomic treat and a special moment for the family's relationship. 'At home, I was taught that food was sacred and should be treated with humility, respect and honesty,' Bittor stresses.

His bond with the land, his devotion to his kin and the solemnity of the daily gastronomic act awakened in him, at a very young age, a fascination with the restaurant industry. This was shaped during his holidays in Bilbao on visits to his maternal cousins whose family ran a bar and an eatery where wine was served with the dish of the day. 'It remained etched in my mind. I saw it as something social and as a pleasure, rather than a way of making a living,' he explains. The dream of having his own restaurant took shape when he was young. But, back then, if you were born in a rural environment and your family didn't have the means, your only option was to stay on the farm. Only if you found a job at one of the nearby factories could you choose to have a better life. With the idea of working as soon as possible to help his family, Bittor did his military service as soon as he turned eighteen. After 14 months in the Canary Islands he returned, finding his first job away from the farm, as an unskilled worker paving paths and roads. Not long after, he worked in a factory in Apatamonasterio that made cardboard trays. Almost ten years went by before he bought Etxebarri.

Bittor had inquired about the edifice that is now home to Etxebarri in Axpe, who name means 'new house' in Euskera. The building was about three hundred years old and, in its day, was a private home with a structure similar to its current one, although it was actually two homes and housed livestock as well. Years later it was turned into a corner shop and a tavern where they also served food. Due to its location in the centre of Axpe, next to the town hall, the church of Saint John and the *fronton* court, it was the heart of the village during Bittor's youth.

Those were difficult days for the Arginzoniz family – and for their neighbours – as they knew no other routine than that of spending the week working with their livestock on the farms in the area. But if you wanted to socialise, Etxebarri was the only place that served wine. Everyone met up there: those who emerged from mass with those who got together for a drink, those who came to buy provisions with those who got together to play cards. Sunday, after mass, was the big day. Basque *pelota* was played on the *fronton* court and there were stone-lifting competitions or races with animals dragging rocks. There was betting every Sunday at Etxebarri and the wine always flowed.

In the early 80s and following the death of one of its owners, Etxebarri's restaurant business had to close. Bittor bought the building in 1989 after it had been closed for almost a decade. His paternal uncles, Andrés and Patxi – a monk and priest, respectively – to whom Bittor was very close, made a considerable contribution by lending him the money to purchase the place. Bittor, at the age of just twenty-eight, was now the proprietor of his own grill-house.

The surroundings were magical: next to the family farmhouse where he grew up, in the heart of the Atxondo Valley, flanked by the peaks of the mythological Anboto, in touch with the nature that he so loved, and surrounded by his people. All bonds that link him to his roots, to his family, to his childhood memories. However, Etxebarri, this big rambling building that was three hundred years old, was in need of renovation from top to bottom. 'The structure was more or less the same, except for the current terrace that was the home's vegetable garden. Inside, halfway down the hall, was the corner shop, and just before it was the bar. On the right were two small dining rooms and at the back was the kitchen.'

The house was in ruins. It was gutted and only the outer walls were left standing. Bittor took advantage of skills he had learned on an industrial course on electrical wiring to re-do – with his own hands – the electrical installation. He also did the cast-iron work and the roof. It was a gargantuan task: He worked seven days a week and, as soon as he could, he moved in so that he could devote himself completely to making his dream come true. The work was done in record time, beginning on May 1, 1989, and finishing on April 27, 1990.

The first years at Etxebarri were very demanding. The premises went from being a village bar where food was occasionally served, to a traditional grill-house that opened every day with two meal services four days a week, and one on the other three. Bittor, who had no culinary training nor experience in the restaurant industry, didn't cook and, at the start, ran the place, hiring a cook and two helpers. He made up for that lack with total dedication: he would answer the phone, confirm bookings and take orders, serve fish soup to diners, prepare the bills, and deal with suppliers.

When he was about thirty, the daily struggle to keep his restaurant going became clear to Bittor. Back then, when lunch service was over, he would hike up to the peak of the Anboto – over 1,200 metres high – three times a week, and be back in time for the evening service. A witness to this hectic pace was Patricia Velar, first when she was a waitress, and then as Bittor's girlfriend. And then in 1999 as his wife and mother of their two children. 'Even then he had an extraordinary sense of duty. Nothing came before the restaurant. That partly explains his success,' says Patricia, who runs the front-of-house staff.

It didn't take long for the restaurant to be warmly received. It was often full, particularly on Saturdays and Sundays. The traditional food of a typical grill-house in that area was most appealing. The first courses were classics: homemade croquettes, portions of ham, clams in green sauce, oven-baked crab, asparagus, stuffed vegetables in an avocado cream sauce, grilled white prawns from Huelva, roasted peppers. Popular too were some of their stews and bean dishes such as stewed oxtail, and salt cod, as well as the usual sea bream and nape of hake that were already being grilled over wood coals. But the star dish was, without a doubt, their beef chop that was, at that time, griddled.

However, even before his commitment to wood coals that led to a change in concept and catapulted him to fame, Bittor already knew that he didn't want to be at the helm of just any old grill-house. This was apparent soon after he opened, insisting on serving the bread on a little plate, unlike all the other grill-houses where it was served in a basket. 'If I had wanted to be like everyone else, I wouldn't have opened this restaurant,' he said, decidedly. A true statement of intent that been unfolding over the years: firstly with the charcoal grill, then with wood and finally with his ovens. With a search for superior produce, with his very personal and non-transferable creations. With new utensils and his refined techniques. 'What do I want? What do I need? I do it,' he says.

84

CONTINUES »

'Bittor's childhood in
the family farmhouse
was imbued with the
aromas of the daily stew
mingled with the smoke
of wood coals'

Perfectionism and determination have been hallmarks of the place since the very first day. But it is fire that has been the true catalyst of Etxebarri's evolution since 1995. That was the year that the gradual transformation of cooking with gas to one based on wood coals began to take shape, and the moment when Bittor started to be in charge in the kitchen. The turning point came when a barbecue was installed outside the kitchen; but the revelation came when he first cooked a beef chop over the wood coals. It was a gastronomic discovery of huge significance. 'I realised that the chop was not the same as when it was griddled. It was chalk and cheese, something completely different. It couldn't be compared in any way at all,' Bittor remembers.

Seeing the potential of what wood coals could do, Bittor threw himself into experimenting. He started grilling the first fish: sea bream, hake necks. He also explored with other meat and fish, or what his customers asked him to try. Almost everything that he grilled was successful, so what was grilled over wood coals never saw a griddle again. The enthusiastic reception in the dining room confirmed that he was on the right track. Swept along by this change in approach, it was he who, definitively, took over at the helm of the grill. As it happened, at that time there were no cooks who knew how, or wanted, to work at a grill and so it was during this transition to grilling over wood coals that Bittor became a full-time cook.

But this new energy that he wanted to imbue in his menu was stymied by Etxebarri's logistical shortcomings. The kitchen did not meet the requirements needed to give the grill the leading role he wanted, mainly because the only working barbecue at the time was not large enough to cater to the entire restaurant. The fact that it was outdoors didn't help: if it was windy, it ended up on the ground, and if it rained things were even worse. Bittor decided to have the area where he would do the grilling covered and extended, improvements that allowed him to continue experimenting with new ingredients as he mastered others that he had worked on before.

It was then when it dawned on him that he needed to expand the variety and quality of the raw materials he was working with. The wood coals made Bittor look at what came from the sea in another light as until then it had not been so important. It wasn't just that what he offered couldn't be served with a sauce; it was that grilling over wood coals is clean and, because of that, the quality – good and bad – of the produce is more apparent, a rule that is even starker with fish and shellfish. And so, the change to wood coals forced Bittor to find suppliers of the best produce possible, a quest that over the years has grown into an obsession. A decisive factor was swapping oak charcoal for wood, and was pivotal for endowing his culinary creations with elegance, aromas and finesse.

This decision can be attributed to the person who has most inspired Bittor throughout his career: the food critic, Rafael García Santos.

They met in 1995 and from the following year onwards García Santos has decisively contributed to the haute-cuisine revolution at Etxebarri. Captivated by his creative style, his culinary daring and upright, genuine character, García Santos took part in Bittor's countless culinary activities. He was a witness to his way of cooking, tasted his creations and delivered his verdict. He determined whether a dish made sense, if it was overcooked, or if there were technical errors. Bittor remembers that he was very critical, but also that he learned a lot. 'His input was essential. If I hadn't had someone like him at hand, I wouldn't have been able to cook in this way. Without him I wouldn't have seen things that he got me to see,' he recognises.

The conceptual and technical foundation that García Santos instilled in him was, needless to say, priceless, in particular for a cook without culinary training who had learned to cook via feelings. But equally important was the moral support for Bittor who – completely alone and with the determination of one who is self-taught – had committed himself to a style of cooking on which practically nothing had been written as nobody was doing it. García Santos thus became the great confessor and a source of inspiration for Bittor on his journey to the unknown world of grilling over wood coals. He was the crucial travelling companion whose criticism guided the way.

One of his first contributions was to suggest a change of fuel: from charcoal, that was dirtier and invasive, to different woods that were more natural and aromatic. From there sprang the idea that it was key to have total control over the wood coals: that the hearth should be managed by using a separate oven so that live coals would be on hand at all times to be taken from the oven to the grill, thus roasting each item with just the right amount of embers. It worked. In 1997 the first wood oven in Etxebarri's kitchen was finished.

The high temperatures made this wood oven crack inside. The same things happened to the second one, made of volcanic stone. They got it right using fire bricks and today's ovens will last forever. In any case, the decision to adapt the kitchen to give the oven a bigger role coincided with Bittor's firm belief that wood coals were going to be the unquestionable star of what he offered on his menu. Consequently, and with the right infrastructure, he really took off: he put whatever fell into his hands onto the grill and received García Santos's approval. Etxebarri thus entered its most creative and bold moment: it was the start of a journey to the rarefied atmosphere of the best restaurants in the world.

Bittor had, of course, tried many foods that were not grilled over wood coals; this stemmed from his desire to improve, to recover age-old flavours and offer his customers what he most liked. He made his own Idiazábal cheese and tried curing ham at his farmhouse with the aim of elevating it to gastronomic heights, but abandoned the idea because the natural conditions were not right for curing to perfection. But he was successful in 1995 when he modernised chorizo. He based this on what he had always seen at home, but raised it to a new level of excellence thanks to the use of unparalleled raw materials and improved artisanal technique. In general, the menu of the old grill-house began to shrink as dishes were replaced by new produce or new, better quality ones were added. For example, griddled white prawns from Huelva were supplanted by the more pronounced and elegant red prawns from Palamós that were grilled over wood coals, and totally unknown in Atxondo. As these raw materials influenced the new script, an original practice was introduced that is still followed today: every item, as a rule, is run over the embers to infuse it with smoky nuances and natural aromas, and is what gives Bittor's signature cuisine its unmistakable touch. The perfume of the wood coals has thus become a symbol and the spark of the cuisine at Etxebarri.

The first significant sign of greatness in the kitchen was what Bittor did with anchovies. These most delicate oily fish approach the Cantabrian coast in the spring, having come from the cold waters of the north. They arrive resplendent, with lots of fat and ready to lay their eggs. As a raw material they are undisputed: not only are they local anchovies, but at this time of the year they are at their best. However, they are also very delicate fish, suffering as soon as they are removed from the water, and are very vulnerable to the effect of fire because of their fine skin and the little flesh they have. So, how can they be roasted and still have a fresh taste? Bittor came up with a magical solution: he butterflied and gutted two fish, lay one on top of the other – flesh to flesh – and tied their tails together.

This double-anchovy-in-one, combined with the perfect amount of time over the wood coals, revealed itself to be a true gastronomic revolution. The thicker double fillets, and the gentle effect of the heat from the fire, gave Bittor the answer he was looking for: the perfect balance between cooking and freshness. The result is an unbeatable anchovy, a synthesis of qualities: a raw material at its peak, the pinkness of its flesh, smoky nuances, a creamy texture, and hot all the way through. The magic behind this dish is twofold: on the one hand, Bittor was ingeniously and intellectually brilliant to achieve the complex challenge he had set himself; and, on the other, was his ability to execute his concept with extraordinary technical precision.

This milestone – that marked a turning point for Etxebarri's future – was not the last time that Bittor challenged culinary convention. Doing away with having to cook elvers twice, grilling salt cod over wood coals, or daring to run oysters over the embers (explained further on), are other famous inventions of his. With all these culinary demands, it became necessary to change the approach in the dining room. In 2008 they decided to reduce the eleven weekly meal services to the seven they offer today. This meant that, with the exception of Saturdays, dinners were dropped, and Mondays became a day off for the staff. 'This change was absolutely necessary. It was unworkable to have two meal services with one team working at that crazy pace,' Patricia Velar points out.

After reducing the meal services and being on The World's 50 Best Restaurants for the first time, they introduced their tasting menu in 2008. It was then – having completed the transition from a traditional grill-house – that Etxebarri set their sights on excellence. Over the past decade, its menu has become even more sophisticated with the addition of superior produce and a more culinary touch to its creations, and distinguished with a Michelin star since 2010. Recognition as one on the best restaurants in the world is a just prize for the way it has evolved.

4

The first cracks of light appear dimly in the sky as the new day dawns. The morning is freezing as well as damp, as is usual in winter in the Basque Country. There is a smell of moss and dew, but the smell of burning wood from a nearby chimney can also be distinguished. The cheerless light outside contrasts with the yellowish halo thrown by the light bulbs of the Arginzoniz family farmhouse. Silence reigns between the occasional sounds from the woods. Soon, the murmur of domestic animals can be heard as the day begins: hens, dogs, cats, buffaloes.

Bittor's routines also begin. The diesel engine of his hardy van roars and he heads off to Etxebarri. He opens the doors, takes the bread dough and the fresh cheese, and gets back behind the wheel. Ahead of him is a 10-kilometre drive to a baker's in the municipality of Itzurza where they make artisanal bread. Twenty minutes accompanied by the rhythmic drone of the windscreen wipers. Wrapped in the morning mist, driving on the wet tarmac, dodging the traffic of heavy vehicles coming in the opposite direction. The trip allows Bittor to organise the day in his mind. For two decades this has been part of his daily routine.

Bittor pays tribute to bread made with the artisanal patience and dedication that sourdough and a wood-fired oven require; details that are not trivial. The slow motion of natural fermentation not only condemns industrial yeasts to eternal exile, but it offers – as a counterbalance – a bread rich in flavours and aromatic subtleties topped off by the final touch brought about by being baked in a wood-fired oven. The morning effort that Bittor makes every day is consistent with his way of understanding cooking. His philosophy is crystal clear: produce is sacred. In other words, it must always be the best. The highest expression of finesse, authenticity and flavour.

Bittor clings to this core belief and spares no personal expense in generosity or costs; this means that the most elegant raw materials always take centre stage in his gastronomic project. This fierce defence of produce allows Etxebarri to stand apart at a time when finding excellent raw materials is harder and harder to do, if not impossible. The apparent simplicity of his dishes demands – although this is almost never obvious – an enormous effort starting with the always challenging task of being supplied with the best produce.

With this in mind, Bittor has always avoided ever-tempting shortcuts. It involves, as we said before, going in person to buy artisanal bread at a nearby village every day. It means dedicating his afternoons to the vegetable garden, following up on the beer and his suppliers. It means not delegating when it comes to the latter and, furthermore, requires cultivating a relationship of trust with them that transcends the merely professional and leads to supplies of even higher quality. This has resulted in him driving thousands of kilometres for him to be personally responsible for choosing the produce. These tiny differentiating details to choose only the very best and not just what is good are what set Etxebarri apart.

Emerging from behind this obsession for perfect produce and authenticity of flavour are, needless to say, emotional memories from the past. Sensations surface in Bittor that go back to his childhood on the family farm; flavours, aromas and tastes of when he was little, and the memories of a way of life that was tightly bound to nature. From that time and that place comes his almost mystical respect for produce, only understood when it is at its very best. In other words, the way it has always been. This explains Bittor's devotion to freshness, natural flavour and seasonality, and the reason why this personal legacy comes to life via Etxebarri's menu and clearly influences his cuisine.

His desire for quality produce also stems from a second rationale: fire. This other core pillar of his culinary force obliges him to pay great attention to raw materials. It's logical: the technique of grilling over wood coals is unforgiving.

It doesn't allow for gimmicks, it won't let you embroider the ingredients or hide or disguise them behind foams or sauces. Quite the opposite…fire and wood coals enhance both the greatness and the mediocrity of raw materials, and that of fish and seafood in particular. This meant that Bittor – raised on a farm, quite far from the ocean – had to make a huge effort to fully understand produce from the sea and the secrets of how it was supplied.

And so he did. He was well versed in meat and vegetables, but what came from the sea was unfamiliar to him. 'Fish and seafood were new to me. I had to learn how to buy them. How? By trial and error. By having to throw away a lot of food and wasting a lot of money,' he recalls. Being supplied with the best fish thus became a priority. Three times a week for almost two decades he drove to the fish markets in Ondárroa, Bermeo and Lekeitio, and sometimes even all the way to Santoña, so he could choose. A pilgrimage – made every other day – from Etxebarri to personally inspect the bright eyes and smooth, shiny skin of a particular fish and thus choose the freshest and best quality ones.

His nose for finding good supplies evolved over the years as he learned. Quality was improved upon with each fish that was discarded and with each new supplier. Little by little, his trips to the ports along the Cantabrian coast turned into daily phone calls to his suppliers. They, at the fish market, would list him the most exclusive catches of the day. Anchovies caught at dawn, female turbots about to lay their eggs, magnificent groupers weighing several kilos. 'My suppliers know exactly what I want. And they know that I seek the best,' Bittor stresses. Seasons are also vital because it is important to have the best fish when they are in peak condition and have the most fat: mackerel and anchovies in the spring; red mullet, bonito and tuna in summer; sea bream from September onwards, and grouper in autumn and well into winter.

His achievement is having got his suppliers not to tender, in other words, despite having other customers to satisfy, they set aside all the best that they have and not just part of it. Bittor points to the key in achieving this: trust. Trust that has been built up over years and is the fruit of endless hours of close, personal contact that has forged staunch loyalties. For example, with Lluís Cros, from whom Etxebarri receives a batch of red prawns first thing in the morning that, the previous afternoon, were swimming in the waters of the Costa Brava, hundreds of kilometres from here. They are not your usual prawns and, thanks to their size and quality, are famous for being the most aristocratic of the many varieties available on the market. Their reputation stems from their origins that offer the ideal habitat for crustaceans – the fishing grounds of Rostoll and San Sebastián de Palamós.

The key factor is the small size of both fishing grounds that are hardly more than two kilometres square. Such a small area ensures that boats only fish there for one hour a day at the most; this means that the prawns are in the net for a short time, flapping about and hurting themselves less and, as a result, have firmer flesh. Furthermore, his supplier is scrupulous about the boats he uses and his fishing techniques, factors that result in the freshest red prawns whose texture is exceptional, in addition to being impressive in size: from 18 to 20 prawns per kilo, at about 60 grams per creature.

Lluís also supplies him with sea cucumbers that are firm and meaty, unusual even on restaurant tables and at the main fish markets along the Mediterranean. Baby octopuses also come from him; the best thing about them being where they are sourced: fishing grounds with coarse, sandy sea beds that are quite uncommon. Most baby octopuses from the Mediterranean typically live on sea beds with fine sand, making it bothersome to wash them; even doing them one by one, it is hard to remove every grain of sand. And so, thanks to their own merit, Lluís's baby octopuses are on Etxebarri's menu, together with sea cucumbers and red prawns that are also outstanding.

Sea cucumbers, baby octopuses and red prawns at Etxebarri? At first glance, it seems surprising. One would say that these three supremely Mediterranean delicacies are perhaps out of place. Despite its sophistication, Etxebarri is still a Basque grill-house whose cuisine is mainly Cantabrian in style. A cuisine that is very much of the north, of rough seas and of the land, it abounds with Galician seafood, red meat and salt cod; with elvers, kokotxas and sea bream; woodcock, peppers and pocha beans. But the truth is that, without betraying its hallmarks, Etxebarri is also a place of welcome. The sea cucumbers, baby octopuses and red prawns not only bring a subtle touch of Mediterranean exoticism to the menu, but also means that Bittor does not have gastronomic borders. If the produce makes sense and is elegant, there are no limits.

The same faith that Bittor has in Lluís, he has in Iraeta Viveros, his seafood supplier. For years he would drive all the way to Pasajes, a fishing town close to the French border where Iraeta's fish hatcheries are located. There, he bought lobsters, velvet crabs, brown crabs, langoustines and other seafood. Now, however, the logistics have been simplified. They meet in a lay-by on the AP-8 motorway where the lorry passes every day on its way to Mercabilbao. The handover is quick and routine, almost clandestine. They greet each other, climb into the back of the refrigerated lorry and, under a fluorescent light, choose the seafood from the hatchery. The repertoire is traditional and glorious. Galician, Scottish, Cantabrian. Live, seasonal creatures. Everything is top quality.

CONTINUES »

'Routines also get Bittor going. The diesel engine of his hardy van roars and he heads off to Etxebarri'

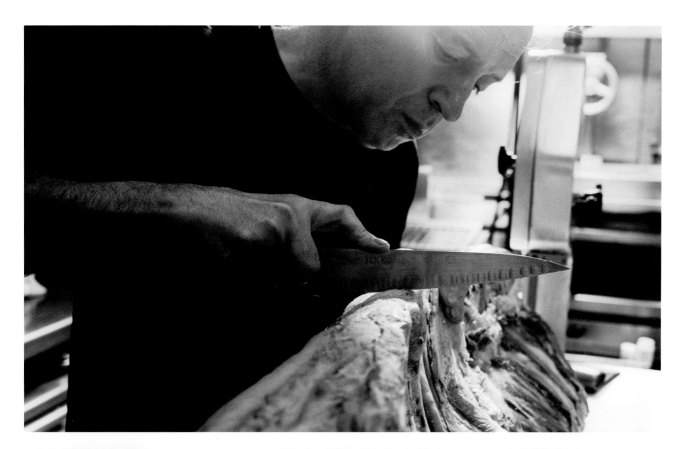

PERSEVERANCE
AND EFFORT

That is the daily challenge for the best produce. But there is no alternative: Bittor accepts that the threshold of excellence of his menu forces him to be very demanding when it comes to choosing raw materials. The same goes for little morsels like his chorizo, whose artisanal process of production requires incredible dedication despite the fact that on the menu it is just an amuse-gueule. Thus, the pork chosen for it is the best; acorn-fed Iberico pork from Joselito. Bittor refines the choice even further, only using the most special parts of the animal: 'presa' pork shoulder and meat from the 'Secreto' cut.

But it is not enough to choose the best animal and the most tender meat; it also has to be recently slaughtered and must be transported at a low temperature. It then undergoes a painstaking artisanal process with a marinade of choricero peppers from his own farm. A variety of pepper that requires constant care from when it is planted at the start of spring, to end with its drying at the beginning of autumn and well into winter. Everything could, of course, be simplified. But these animals that feed on acorns on the hillsides of Extremadura, the special cuts of meat, and the peppers from this terroir are what make Etxebarri's chorizo unique and a delicacy.

Sure, we have seen how Bittor's farm is something vital for him, his point of reference. But, as in the case of the peppers, it is also an unlimited pantry of local produce the quality of which cannot be bought at the market. Other farmed produce needed daily at Etxebarri thus has to pass a thorough test. The enemy is the artificial touch of refrigeration that contaminates vegetables: each station in the kitchen goes over the kind of produce received. Everyone is clear about what the standard of quality is. The price is not the most important factor, quality is. If the produce does not pass muster, it is returned. If it is not perfect, they don't want it.

Excellence, furthermore, demands an extra dose of meticulousness. For example, clams can only come from Galicia, the indisputable best, but, among those, Etxebarri chooses the type with the best attributes: Palourde clams that weigh 40 grams each. Likewise, porcini in autumn, and St George's mushrooms (known locally as *perretxikos*) in spring and summer, must not only be from Urkiola because they are more perfumed, but because they prefer the ones from the peaks to those of the slopes. As with everything, sophistication has its own name: Asturian salmon. As it is rare, it is a gastronomic treasure. A luxury for those that are chosen. A museum piece. Only occasionally is it on the menu. Those from other places don't cut the mustard and are rejected.

THE PRODUCE

It might go unnoticed by most diners, but the supply of other, more common, raw materials on the menu, in truth, involve a huge challenge. Sourcing beef chops is a particular example. It is one of the classic items at any self-respecting grill-house – above all in the Basque Country – where red meat is a religion. But this carnivorous tradition is out of step with the reality of the ever lower quality of meat, and obliges Bittor to search high and low. He prefers the Galician Blond breed crossed with other kinds as the marbling of the meat – a key factor for juiciness and flavour – is better in mixed breeds. But it is not easy to find animals which, in addition to being between eight and ten years old, have been fed on grass and corn, and have been humanely slaughtered.

It was just as arduous to find a trustworthy supplier of goat's milk with which to make the restaurant's butter. If the complicated aspect of the chops is finding the right ones among the excessive supply that has devalued those of even average quality, the difficulty related to goat's milk lies in its scarcity. Goats are complicated creatures and hard to domesticate and, combined with a small market, explains why raising them is gradually waning. The production of goat's milk is therefore relatively small and, to make matters worse, what there is, is almost totally used to make cheese. So, in addition to his supplier in Yurre, in the Arratia-Nervión district in Álava, Bittor continued to search until he found a farmer in León who, since then, has supplied him with another 75 litres of milk each week, delivered to Etxebarri in isothermal containers and with the proper cold chain.

The buffaloes on his farm are also the result of his fascination with perfect produce. 'Their milk is lighter and healthier, perfect for making fresh cheese. But you can't wait when it comes to milk, it has to be very fresh to do things properly, especially when making mozzarella. What truly makes a difference is having milk that has just been milked that morning,' Bittor explains. To achieve this he invested almost three years, travelled to the Italian region of Campania twice, learned the secrets of making mozzarella from a local cheese maker, overcame all kinds of obstacles and ended up setting off on the odyssey of transporting two buffaloes from southern Italy to his farm in Atxondo. An enormous effort the rewards of which can be tasted in Etxebarri's various fresh-cheese recipes.

But perhaps the produce that gave Bittor the biggest headache was salt cod. Just like the chops, kokotxas and peppers, salt cod is one of the most iconic elements of Basque gastronomy. Some years ago, his salt cod came from the Faroe Islands; the pieces were large and meaty with lots of fat, and full of gelatine that made it versatile to grill over wood coals. Quality was very much linked to its natural curing in sheds that lasted months, until the standardization of the drying process substituted sheds for saline injections, allowing the process to be shortened and leading to a massive change in the quality of salt cod.

In fact, cutting the curing time to less than half of what it was – in order to sell more – has been detrimental to the product. When it is hydrated to desalt it, it needs to be eaten shortly after as it soon begins to smell and taste strange, and then goes off. It also suffers when cooked over wood coals as its flavour has diminished and has become chewy in texture. During this whole saga, Bittor looked for suppliers in Norway and Iceland that could guarantee naturally dried salt cod, but if the decline continued, he would have to take the dish off the menu despite it being a hallmark of his cuisine.

That would be a disaster for him because in 2004 he was among the first to grill this iconic gastronomic ingredient of the Basque Country, that, until then had only been cooked in a pilpil or Vizcaina sauce. Grilling it seemed sacrilegious, almost a provocation, but his creation soon garnered general recognition. Seen as something original, diners above all appreciated its cleaner taste, its succulent texture and the hint of smoke from the wood coals. 'People really liked it. One of the dishes that most captivated diners,' Bittor explains.

What not all of his diners know is, that to reach that level of excellence, Bittor not only went to great lengths to be supplied with a raw material that measured up, but that he had to experiment thousands of times and invest countless hours to achieve the perfect cooking time that would bring the best out of the fish. If the flesh didn't flake well, it was no good. If the heat didn't penetrate properly, he wasn't satisfied. If the loss of gelatine made it too dry, he discarded it. Dozens, if not hundreds, of salt cod fillets went straight into the rubbish bin. But Bittor didn't waver; he put his perfectionism and stubbornness at the service of the cause and didn't give up until he got the salt cod he wanted; a combination of unquestionable raw material and surgically precise cooking.

This union of produce at its best plus a perfect way of cooking it is the hallmark of another of the restaurant's iconic dishes: elvers. Elvers are special creatures: gastronomically unique, rare and with a short season. And so, bearing that in mind, Bittor forced himself to give his all to this delicacy. An haute-cuisine concept, one of the most innovative and, perhaps, the most original of those conceived at Etxebarri, was to do away with the second cooking of the elvers. Traditionally, they are cooked twice: boiled to conserve them, and then sautéed when the recipe requires them to be hot. For Bittor, this is a mortal sin. Some time ago he had the original idea of making a fine-mesh metal pan; he also has a tank at the restaurant to keep the elvers alive, doing away with the need to boil them.

He then sprays them with oil and sautées them over the wood coals the aroma of which spectacularly replaces the traditional way they are sautéed in

Bilbao with oil, garlic and chilli. Not only because they do not need to be cooked twice – an extraordinary feat in itself – but because sautéeing in hot oil softens the elvers, and their flavour is somewhat masked by the garlic and chilli, but, when they are cooked over wood coals they retain all their characteristics. In other words, with their own salinity, with a much firmer texture and decidedly less fatty. The icing on the cake of this incredible process – that perfects an already sublime raw material – is the aroma of the embers.

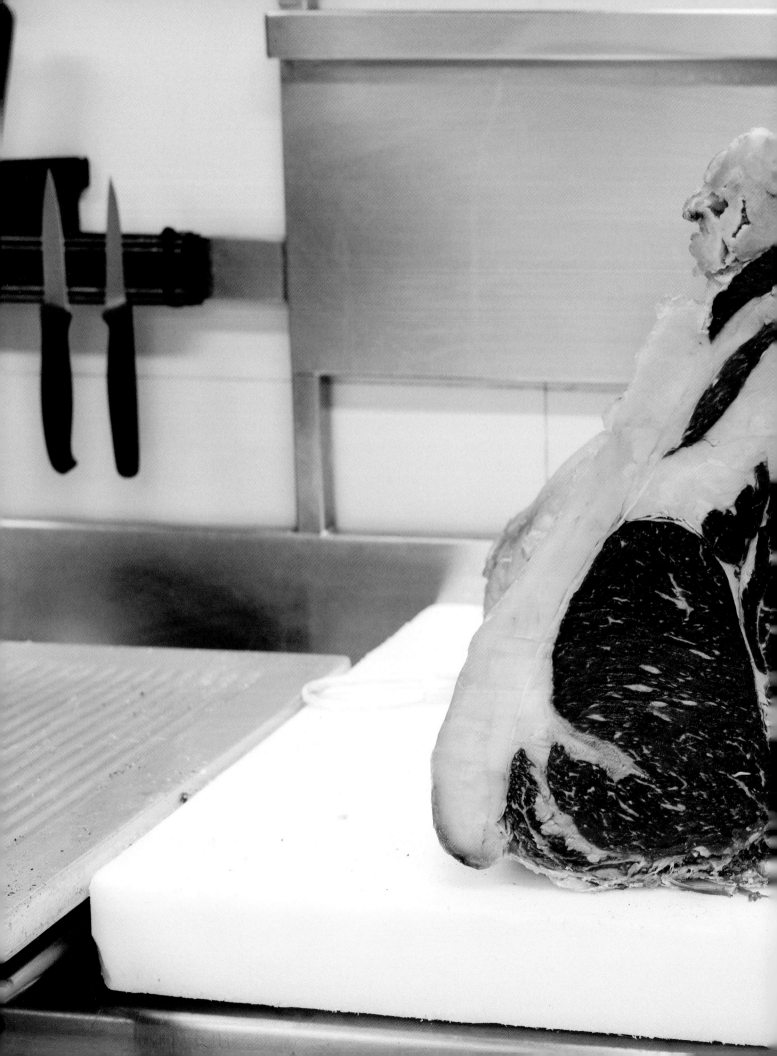

5

Dressed all in black, Bittor mops the drops of sweat that trickle down his brow and allows himself a fleeting moment of respite from the grill. He takes a step back from the fire, but keeps his eye firmly on it. From here, he silently observes with his clinical eye how a piece of salt cod is doing as it is grilling over the wood coals. He watches how it changes colour, how the gelatine sparks as it drips onto the coals, how the heat penetrates to the core of the fillet. And the thread of smoke given off by the oak as it burns. The wood coals are absolute precision: there is no room for error or slip-ups. Fire imposes its magic or cruelty along a fine line that separates perfection from nothingness.

Replicating the uncompromising ways of the fire is culinary micro-surgery. Bittor is aware of this and so faces his duel with the wood coals with the skill of an attacking fencer. Distance, concentration and strategy. Geometry, observation and patience. Intuition, skill and art. All qualities used to master the wood coals with the simple goal of grilling the produce – free from any condiment, sauce or seasoning – in its own juices, thus revealing its purity and natural flavour. It is a cuisine that is easy to comprehend but difficult to execute. A cuisine of feeling that requires an exhaustive understanding of the anatomy of the produce and, at the same time, a special sensitivity to master the fire.

Based on commitment and passion, Bittor has transformed grilling into an art. He had no need to resort to scientific formulas or modern technology, nor experiment with what is called molecular gastronomy, or even challenge the limits of haute cuisine. On the contrary, he has rejected cooking that looks towards the future and has set his eye on the past: on traditional flavours, on the daily fire of the family's hearth, on the origins of humankind itself. Together with the most primitive culinary technique, honed after cooking on a razor's edge for two decades, Bittor has achieved a spectacular result: a refined cuisine that is close to perfection.

Hypnotised by the grill, Bittor talks to the fire in a wordless dialogue with no intermediaries, dominating it as our ancestors did hundreds of thousands of years ago. It is the same fire that turned man into human after, according to Greek mythology, the Titan Prometheus stole the sacred fire from the gods to give it to humanity. The precious gift of fire from the gods or, more prosaically, its discovery perhaps following a bolt of lightning, an erupting volcano, or a chance forest fire, marked – together with writing – the most important evolutionary and cultural advance for humankind. Fire was essential for human survival, and learning to master it meant being able to take on nature and improve life in general.

Without fire, our species would have been condemned to live like any other wild animal. It was fundamental for protection against the cold, as defence against predators, to have light when it was dark, and as a weapon for hunting; but, above all, it changed what was eaten. Before mastering fire, primitive humans ate raw meat that, at the most, was warmed in the sun. Mastering fire was key to leaving this wild state behind. Humans not only learned to roast their prey, whose meat became more flavoursome and tender, but many plants, tubers, cereals and pulses that could not be eaten raw, became edible. Controlling fire meant that metals could be worked; this led to the production of utensils and tools, and later clay and ceramic pots that allowed foods to be heated, cooked, boiled and roasted. Thanks to all of this, fire managed to gather around it the members of the group, thus becoming the focal point of the communal hearth and of social life.

Fire was so important for the human diet that many theories exist linking the secret of the evolution of our species to the emergence of cooking. According to some, fire softens meat tissue and makes its nutrients more easily assimilated; this would have been key in reducing the time humans needed to chew and digest foods, allowing our ancestors to spend less time searching for and digesting food and, as a result, could move away from a wild life and employ that time doing other things that fostered their progress. But not just that: the increase in energy obtained from cooked meat was a key reason behind humans developing bigger brains.

Bittor's cooking is, therefore, an atavistic cuisine that, in a way, returns us to our origins. When he stole the secret of fire from the gods, Bittor set in motion a gastronomic choreography that, over the years, has resulted in an ancestral cuisine that makes perfect sense. Fire, animals and nature are, for him, as they were for primitive humans, the elements that influence what he offers every day when he lights the fire in the ovens at Etxebarri. An act that requires dry firewood and a spark to illuminate this high-voltage cuisine.

For Bittor, firewood is, needless to say, congenial territory. Firewood had always been gathered on the hills near Axpe to provide fuel for the family farmhouse, and was the only source of heat. In his youth, he cleaned and reforested the woods, felled trees with an axe and dragged firewood every day, helping him to gain remarkable knowledge about different kinds of wood and in particular about the resin that each one secretes. This is a very important factor from a culinary standpoint because this natural secretion can give off very aggressive aromas, overpowering foods and is irreconcilable with the elegance with which Bittor endows his cooking over wood coals.

Charcoal was not much better. It was the fuel used at Etxebarri when, at the very start, only chops and sea bream were grilled. Charcoal was used until Bittor realised that carbonisation was lethal, making everything dirty and masking flavours beyond recognition; until he realised that firewood was better suited to the subtlety required at Etxebarri because its mild, natural aromas enhanced the flavour of foods. The most valuable for culinary use is, without a doubt, oak. As it burns, its sap – that is high in sugars – gives off clean, perfumed fragrances that go particularly well with raw materials such as fish and seafood.

Meats, on the other hand, can handle more pronounced aromas, and so Bittor prefers to use vine roots together with vine cuttings that burn faster but that contribute more fragrance. Like a perfumer who follows the trail of a specific scent, Bittor also discovered that the wood of fruit trees was ideal for wild salmon and caviar: the citrusy touch of orange for the former, the fresh taste of apple for the latter. And snails, on the menu in winter when it's the season for them, are paired with smoke from straw. They are first blanched and then grilled on a base of straw embers. Despite the fleeting action of the flame, the molluscs are warmed through and are infused with a pronounced flavour of the countryside.

His supplier of firewood is a woodsman from Mendaro – a nearby town in the province of Guipúzcoa – who delivers a batch of oak firewood four times a year. After unloading the lorry, Bittor thanks the woodsmen by offering them a breakfast of fried eggs with chorizo, and often roast lamb...at 7 o'clock in the morning. The vine cuttings come from La Rioja, or from a closer area where Txakoli grapes are grown.

Whichever firewood he uses, Bittor always makes sure that it is perfectly dry; this means that it must have been cut at least a year earlier and stored in a well-ventilated place. This is vital not only because dry wood reaches higher temperatures and so burns faster and more easily, but also because damp wood creates much more smoke, an important issue that cannot be overlooked: while woodsmoke offers a subtle perfume that highlights the virtues of the produce, too much uncontrolled smoke simply masks the taste and distorts its characteristic flavours. This is why – since the first years when he used very lively wood coals – Bittor has reduced the exposure of foods to smoke.

However, a great deal of smoke gets his blessing when the goal *is* to smoke: for example, goat's milk or fish; among the latter is scorpion fish – first lightly marinated and then smoked – and served with a courgette salad in summer. This technique involves the produce being infused with the smoke, but not heated by it. A variation on this technique, although a very subtle one, is applied to Asturian or Cantabrian salmon when in season, a fabulous dish that is not always on Etxebarri's menu due to its scarcity. After cleaning and filleting, it is dry-marinated with orange and lemon zest, fennel and salt, and is then immersed in olive oil for 2 hours.

It is then filleted as for sashimi and placed in a closed wooden box in which is a little container with a live wood coal, dried lemon peel and chamomile in it. The salmon is exposed to this aromatic smoke for just a few moments, the time it takes to carry the plate from the kitchen to the diner. But the result is an extraordinary salmon with a subtle hint of citrus together with the aroma from the live coal. In every other case, the aromatised smoke from the wood coals is applied cautiously, almost reverentially, subtly caressing the food and completing the dish with an additional touch of magic. Milk, eggs, meat and oily fish and, in general, foods that have a high fat content, are those that best – and most quickly – absorb the aroma of the wood.

But aside from the aromatic properties of the various woods, it is vital to be in total control of the wood coals to get the best results from an unpredictable way of cooking such as that done over fire. Long-lasting, consistent woods such as oak obviously make this task easier. However, what is truly

CONTINUES »

'Distance, concentration and strategy. Geometry, observation and patience. Intuition, skill and art'

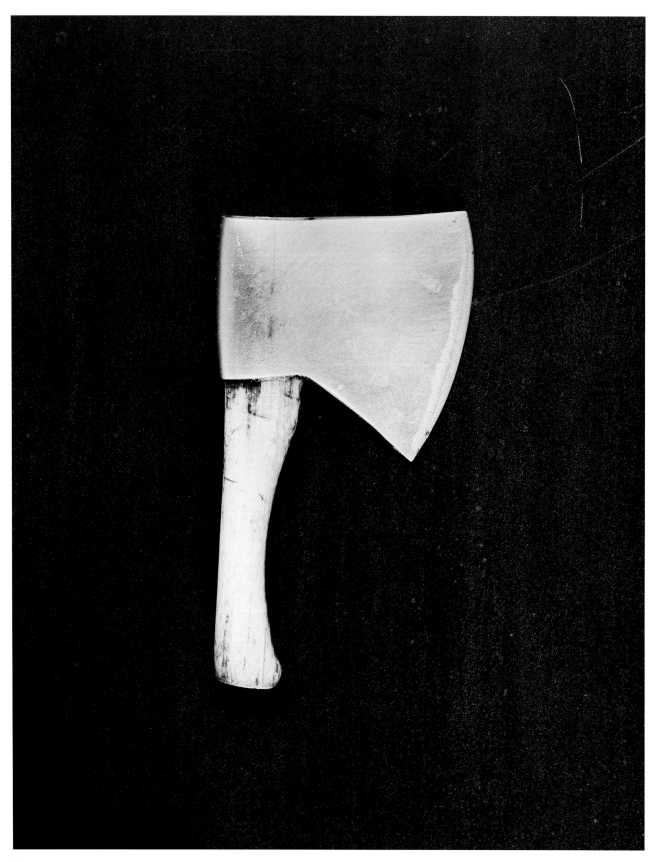

Axe
For cutting beef chops.

Bittor's knives

Shovel for the wood coals
Essential for deciding on how much wood coal
to use for each grill.

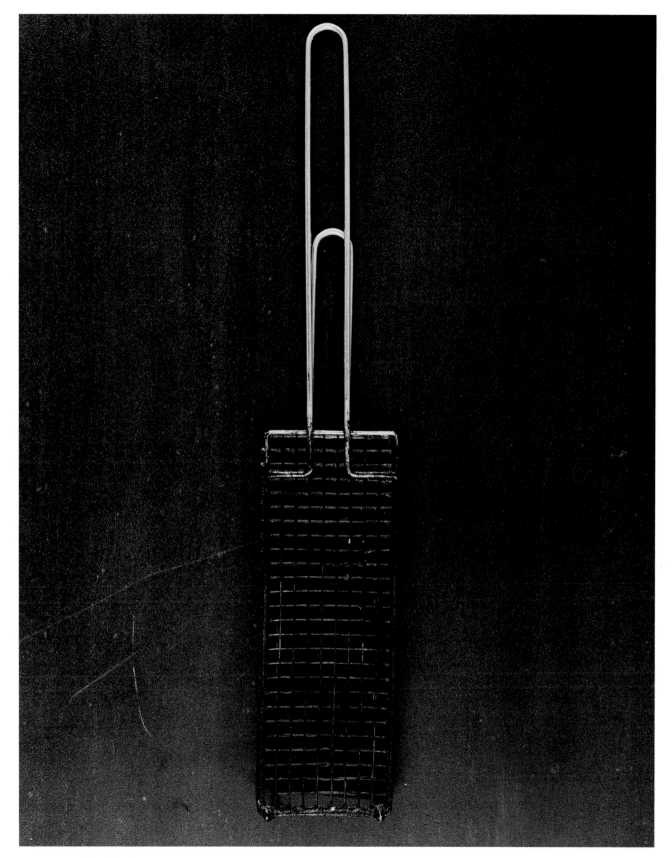

Narrow grilling basket
For anchovies, small fish and, in general everything
that needs to be turned so it can be grilled on both
sides. Flat grilling basket.

Wide, square grilling basket
For turbot and small cod.
Flat, curveless grilling basket.

'Besuguera' grilling basket
Traditional, fish-shaped curved utensil.
For sea bream and medium-large fish.

Titanium grilling basket
The important thing about this is the titanium
as it avoids croquettes and other breaded foods
sticking to the grill.

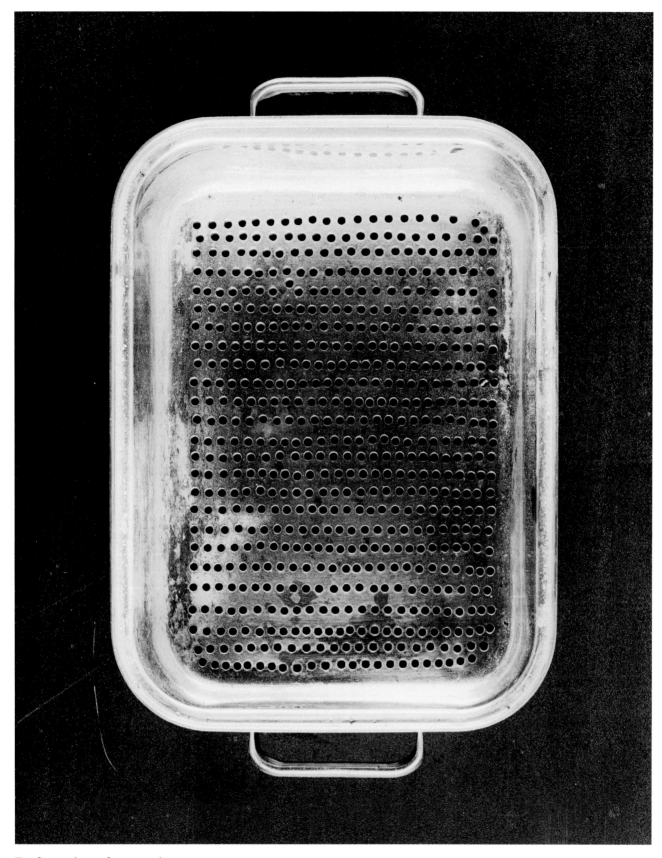

Perforated tray for steaming

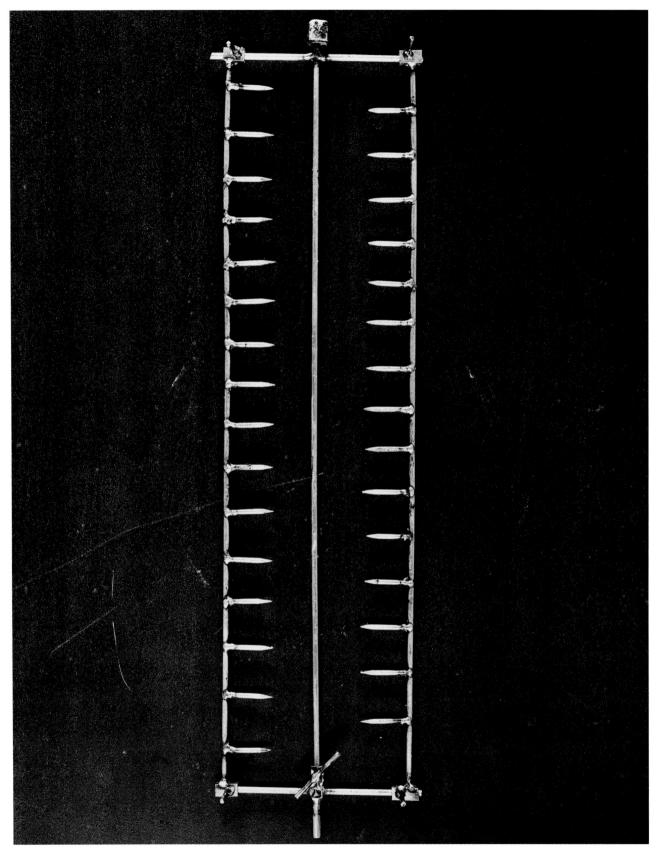

Pronged skewer
For grilling birds.

Very fine-mesh metal pan
For elvers and teardrop peas.

Open-mesh metal pan
For sautéing wild mushrooms or ingredients that need
a high fire, such as baby octopuses. It is undulated and, as
it is more in contact with the fire, needs to be durable.

Pan with laser-made holes
Paella-pan with micro perforations on its base.
For rice dishes.

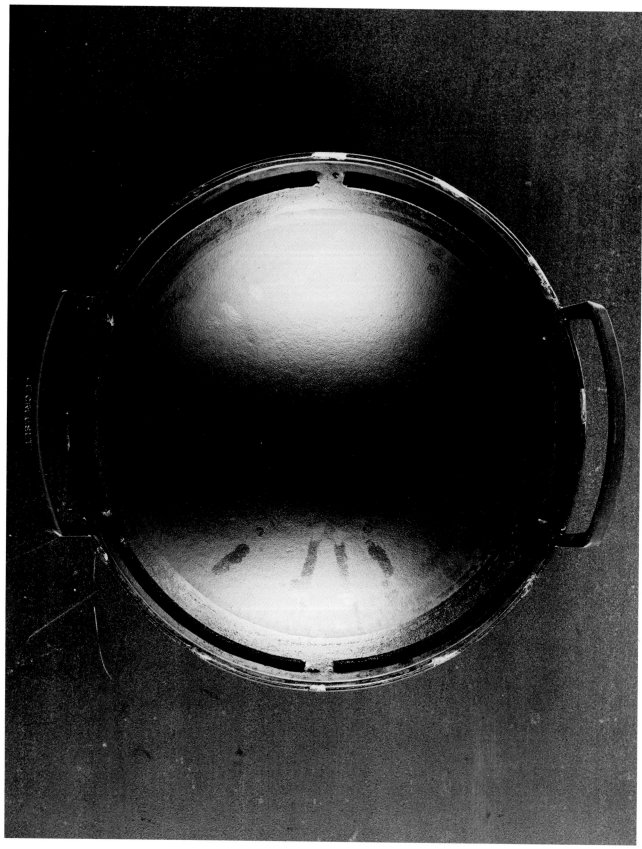

Wok
For frying peppers in tempura batter, snakelocks
anemones, etc.

Poker
To remove the embers and fan the fire.

important is having the proper infrastructure. Bittor came to this conclusion thanks to the stubbornness of his own experience as during the first years he made the wood coals in a corner of the same grill where he cooked his dishes. This meant that he had to work at very high temperatures, juggling miraculously so that he was never short of wood coals, could control the smoke, and so that the embers provided the exact degree of heat demanded by each dish.

The solution he came up with was to have two Moorish-style ovens built in the kitchen next to the grill, not really with the aim of cooking in them but to use them to make wood coals. Despite the fact that they are made with fire bricks (the most resistant material among those that can withstand high temperatures), continuous exposure to 800°C means that they have to be lit on alternate days to avoid them cracking. While the residual heat from the previous day's oven is used to confit, for example, peppers and aubergines, or to roast kid, the second oven devours firewood from first thing in the morning so that Bittor will have enough wood coals for the meal service.

Having a separate space in which to make and prepare the wood coals was an absolute revolution. Above all because it means that the right amount of wood coals can be used for each dish. The exact amount of wood coals are thus taken from the oven to the grill as needed for each ingredient, allowing Bittor to choose from a range of coals with different degrees of heat: from glowing, bright red coals that radiate intense heat for items that require a fast but extreme fire, to dying coals that are white and ashy, pale and consumed, for items that just need a touch of fire. He thus achieves the first requirement for tackling this very untameable way of cooking: mastering the heat given off by the coals.

The second is also to be able to control the height at which the food is cooked over the fire. To do the equivalent of turning up or down the flame on a gas stove, Bittor invented a number of stainless steel and titanium grills that, thanks to a simple system of pulleys, can be raised or lowered depending on how far or close the produce needs to be from the fire. These removable grills are cleaned every day with acid, heat and soap to remove all traces of smells, charred remains and any fat. Bittor points out that the secret of his cuisine is, precisely, to have control over the wood coals, 'It is key to keep an eye on times and temperatures. That can only be achieved with great dedication. It's not a technique that can be taught. It is acquired through years of experience over the wood coals.'

It is not, in fact, at all scientific. It is an artisanal and subjective technique, one that is personal and non-transferable. An art that Bittor has mastered thanks to his innate sensitivity, intuition and perfectionism. Due to his passion, discipline and culinary stubbornness. But adapting his cuisine to cooking over fire

THE FIRE

and tackling the challenges of such risky gastronomic ideas required a steep learning curve. First off, a declaration of war to any dehydration of the produce. And then with height; a mission to endow all food with the perfect point of doneness has obliged him to reduce its exposure to the fire to ensure all the succulence of the produce. And with continuous trial and error: lively or low wood coals, a higher or lower grill, more or less time; everything is done instinctively without a thermometer or a timer. Just with feeling. The godsent madness of the alchemist.

When it comes to grilling, an unparalleled example of his mastery of timing are his runny eggs. Scientifically speaking, the only thing that stops an egg from setting is to cook it at less than 65°C. But to make that happen over wood coals, gently stirring the eggs so that they do not set but become creamy is, without a doubt, an example of superb precision. Via the execution of this recipe, Bittor has shown his ability to apply – with nothing other than his clinical eye – concepts of haute cuisine, such as a mathematical control of temperature, to his cooking over wood coals. In fact, such a singular cuisine required Bittor to design utensils, right from the very start, that would adapt to the cuisine he championed. He had to invent utensils that didn't exist because Bittor cooks in an unconventional way. The narrow grilling basket came about when he decided to grill anchovies, the wok for frying peppers in tempura batter, and the modified pan for warming caviar, among other produce.

The mussel pot was devised when he realised that putting mussels on the grill made them lose all their liquid, depriving them of most of their juiciness and flavour. So Bittor invented a utensil with a lid that would retain the mussels' juices and, at the same time, would allow the aroma of the wood coals to infuse them. The ingenious culinary device keeps the mussels flavoursome, and they are enhanced by a hint of aroma from the wood coals. It is a specific utensil that Bittor designed without any references: he bought a new saucepan and asked a local artisan to cut out a circle in the bottom and solder a metal neck in its place; the aroma and the heat of the wood coals could enter through the funnel creating steam from the liquid of the mussels themselves.

The process is always the same for this and other utensils that Bittor has designed. First, he tries with an existing utensil and imagines how it can be modified to make it just right; then, he has it made and tests this initial version, making the necessary modifications. This was how he conceived the perforated metal-mesh pan with tiny holes so that elvers and teardrop peas could gently roll on its surface without sticking, becoming damaged, or breaking. The micro-perforated pan for rice turned out to be an even greater innovation. Its bottom has such tiny holes they can hardly be seen: they prevent the loss of liquid but are big enough for the aromas from the fire to enter. Onions can be sweated in the pan and the rice can then be gently cooked so that it absorbs the flavour of the wood coals. Once the prawns and lobster have been added, a thick seafood stock is poured in; the rice is stirred as it cooks to make it creamy.

All the utensils were made by an artisan blacksmith in Irún who worked with stainless steel and who, before retiring, made them by hand following his client's instructions. Bittor would drive there to show him a drawing, give him a saucepan to be modified or explain in detail what kind of utensil he needed. The blacksmith would get down to work and, with these various improvements, would come up with the desired utensil. It was he who made the double grill a reality: a conventional grill for roasting chops with a drawer – and a cover – above it to hold wood coals so that the heat would flow downwards. The advantage of this utensil is that it allows the underside of the meat to sear while the top is heated, avoiding a loss of meat juices and making the meat even more flavoursome.

Despite its innovativeness, Bittor only uses this grill from time to time as it is not practical when having to serve a full dining room. Coming up with novel utensils has allowed Bittor to develop his cuisine with far-reaching results as said tools have served as a vehicle for cooking foods on the grill. This led him to invent a conventional grill made of an unusual material – titanium – in order to be able to fry foods over wood coals without them sticking to the grill. His delicate, breaded croquette, for example, is sprayed with oil and placed on this grill so that it fries over the wood coals.

6

ACTION

As midday approaches, the activity in Etxebarri's kitchen accelerates but does not set itself to cruising speed until an hour later. From first thing in the morning, work is relaxed with all team members focusing on their routines and preparations but, when the time for the meal service comes around, the revs in Etxebarri's machine room increase. As soon as the first order comes in, shown on a television screen attached to a wall in the kitchen, the team gets going. Everyone is at their station. Communication is minimal and they work almost in silence. Hardly any orders are given: everyone knows their role.

Bittor takes control of fire. Close at hand, and to the side of the six grills are the tools he uses to tame the wood coals. Perforated pans, grills that are less or more open, 'besuguera' grilling baskets and various pots. Tongs, carving forks, knives, spray bottles of oil, cloths to protect his hands from the heat of the fire. Behind him, a quartet of cooks take up their positions at the kitchen table where

In the room next door, there is a hive of activity too. Plates are washed continuously. The star appetizer, little artisanal chorizo morsels, are prepared. A cook gets stuck into the tortuous process of preparing the peppers; first peeling off the burnt skin without wetting his hands, and then cooking them au confit. Saucepans are on the boil for ages: from apples that cook for at least three days to make the syrup for the cheese crème caramel, to old chickens and hens – for the croquettes – that bubble away in milk over a low temperature for 24 hours. Other saucepans steam with the week's innovations: a stock made with beef bones, and one of pig's trotters; both are being tested. A machine grinds cacao beans from Ghana for the bonbon that ends the tasting menu. The astringent beans become aromatic, balanced and smooth after three days.

A batch of chistorra sausages comes off the grill to be served on a 'talo' or flatbread made from dried corn and cooked over the embers. Their place is taken over by a dozen artichokes that have been steamed and blanched in ice. They are placed upside down so that the fragrance of the wood coals infuses them inside. They are then covered so the heat is distributed evenly. The funnel chanterelles that accompany the dish are sautéed next to them in a mesh pan. Both – the artichokes and the mushrooms – come off the grill at the same time. The artichokes are cut in half, seasoned with salt, and hot garlic oil is poured over them; they are plated topped with the mushrooms. The dish is finished off with a few teaspoonfuls of a gelatinous ham stock.

At the same time, the beef chop is almost ready to be turned over. The red-hot wood coals and the slight flame indicate that it has been sealed on one side. The other side of the dark red meat is covered with white salt, while the yellowish fat around it sweats and drips. Bittor shakes off the excess salt, turns the meat over, grills it for a further five minutes and then sets it on the table where it is sliced and served with Batavia lettuce. Next, Bittor turns the wheel to the left to lower the grill until it almost touches the wood coals that are at their peak. He then lays on it a 'besuguera' grilling basket containing a sea bream. The fat drips at once. The coals spark and curls of smoke appear. There is a smell of crispy skin.

When it is almost done, it is placed on a tray and covered with another one. Its orange tail sticks out. A couple of minutes later, Bittor uncovers it, opens the fish by cutting it from head to tail and lifts the spine out easily. The flesh is shiny and juicy, cooked to perfection. Estela then takes over, pin boning the fish to remove the tiniest bones one by one. She seasons it lightly with salt and pushes the tray to one side for Héctor to plate. He finishes the dish by adding an emulsion of fried olive oil, garlic and hot chilli with rhubarb water that adds a touch of acidity and lightens the full flavour of the sea bream. Another dish is ready to take into the dining room.

Fish fumet. Grouper is the fish of choice, with hake a close second. The subtle flavour of a white fish is sought rather than the brininess of rock fish. The heads and bones are used. They are left to soak in cold water in the fridge to bleed and release any impurities. The fish, leeks, onions and carrots are put in a saucepan of cold water and brought to the boil. After an hour the saucepan is taken off the heat and infused with celery and parsley for a further 30 minutes. It is used to make the green sauce for the kokotxas and for the razor clams.

Chicken stock/consommé. Made with old hens and chickens from Bittor's farm, they are slaughtered the same day the stock is prepared. Aside from the chicken, the bones, feet and cartilage of hens are used to make the stock gelatinous, but no offal is used.
Leeks, onions and carrots are also required. Brought to the boil and then simmered at 85°C for 24 hours, the surface is regularly skimmed to remove any impurities. It is strained through muslin. The heat is turned off and celery is added to infuse for 30 minutes. The result is a consommé that is one of the dishes on the tasting menu.

Ham stock. Joselito Iberico ham bones are used from which all the yellow, rancid fat has been removed. They are then blanched three times in cold water to remove any impurities. The fourth time the bones are cooked in cold water, with no added vegetables. Cooked for three hours over a low heat, uncovered, and then removed. When it is cool it is gelatinous and has a very pronounced flavour. It is used for the artichoke and mushroom recipe after having been reheated.

Vegetable stock. Boil carrots, onions and leeks in a saucepan for two and a half hours over a medium heat. It is used to lighten sauces and for cooking certain vegetables, such as broccoli, artichokes, leeks, etc.

Salt cod stock. Salt cod skins are desalted for three days in cold water, with two changes of water a day, or six in total. On the third day the skins are cooked in water, without any vegetables, for three hours. It is then strained and reduced to the desired consistency. This stock provides little flavour but a lot of gelatine which prevents the various emulsions in which it is used from curdling.

COOKING AND INNOVATION

Green sauce. A traditional sauce used for hake kokotxas.

Pilpil sauce. This sauce is used for the salt cod grilled over wood coals with grilled peppers. Crushed garlic and the desalted trimmings of the salt cod loin are cooked au confit for 30 minutes in oil at a low temperature. Next, the salt cod trimmings are removed, the pilpil sauce is thickened and kept at 50°C so that it remains emulsified.

Pea sauce. The pea pods are sautéed over a high heat on the grill and then liquidised. The smoky touch of the pod juice is combined with vegetable stock and used in the teardrop pea recipe.

Red pepper reduction. Red peppers are liquidised raw. The liquid is reduced for four or five hours in a small saucepan over a very low heat so that it caramelises thanks to its own sugars. The resulting reduction, that has a syrupy consistency, is poured over the accompaniment of grilled peppers to make them shiny and provide an additional flavour.

Reduced woodcock stock. A classic woodcock stock, reduced to a sauce-like consistency (see the recipe for woodcock over wood coals).

EMULSIONS

Soy sauce emulsion. Made with salty soy sauce, lemon juice, sunflower oil, olive oil and a reduced stock made from bonito bones. It is emulsified until it is like an eggless mayonnaise. It is used in bonito and tuna recipes as a base on which the bellies are arranged. For the tuna recipe, grated lemon zest is added to the emulsion.

Rhubarb emulsion. The rhubarb is processed and left to drain so that it releases its water. Rhubarb provides acidity and lightens the full flavour of certain fish. For sea bream it is emulsified with garlic and hot red chillies fried in oil.

COOKING AND INNOVATION

Lemon vinegar or Txakoli emulsion. For grouper, an emulsion is made with oil (in which chillies have been macerated) and lemon vinegar. If the fish has a more delicate flavour, a lighter acidic element is used. For turbot, the same oil is emulsified with Txakoli wine.

Oyster emulsion. The Joselito Iberico pork jowl is cut into little pieces and cooked over a very low heat for two hours so that it releases all its fat. It is strained and set aside. It is emulsified with the water from the oysters.

Oil and sweet wine emulsion. Used for the young squid and baby octopus recipes. The squid are plated and the hot oil in which chilli peppers have been macerated is poured over them so that they continue to cook. The residual oil is then emulsified with sweet red wine.

Black truffle jus. To enhance the aroma of truffles and obtain a few drops of jus, the truffle is wrapped in silver foil and put in the oven for five minutes. The jus is used in the artichoke recipe and for the scrambled eggs with black truffle.

REFLECTION

Nothing is left to chance when it comes to Etxebarri's creations. The entire process is demanding and painstaking. Detail, sensitivity, perfection. Bittor is not a formally trained cook. He is, rather, a grill cook; not just any grill cook, but one with an extraordinary ability to see things that others do not, and to instinctively understand nuances. This sensitivity makes him seek perfection in an obsessive way because all he wants it to create recipes for the grill and make them perfectly. Much of this, of course, comes down to superior produce and wood coals, but Bittor adds many other details and nuances. The magic lies in the nuance that he brings to this cuisine of grilling and he has a team that helps him fulfil that.

We have seen, for example, how his supply system works. It is not enough for the produce to be good; it must be the best. Strictly seasonal and, if possible, local. Thus, vegetables and greens are cared for and grown in Bittor's vegetable garden, picked when they are at their peak. Eggs and milk are fresh that day. Beer and chorizo are made artisanally. Chickens and hens are slaughtered to be consumed that day. He knows the origin of his beef, what the animals ate and how they were slaughtered. Elvers, langoustines, lobsters and clams are kept in tanks at Etxebarri in conditions similar to those of the sea. The fish come from rough seas and nearby coasts. They are all glorious specimens.

The technique used is also pure perfection. Wood that best aromatises each ingredient is chosen. The infrastructure of ovens allows him to always have wood coals on hand and, therefore, master the fire. Over time, Bittor has unravelled the mystery of the wood coals. The combination of intuition, a clinical eye and perfectionism have allowed him to master a very emotional and unscientific technique in order to elevate it to gastronomic excellence. All of the above, that requires incredible effort and dedication that is not always obvious to everyone, is – in and of itself – enough to define an astonishing cuisine. An original, honest, authentic cuisine.

Committing himself exclusively to a cuisine of grilling was, perhaps, in its day, a revolution. But rather than great revolutions, Etxebarri has been exposed, since day one, to a constant evolutionary process. Adding new items to its menu, removing others, adjusting cooking times, and designing pioneering utensils to improve the way certain foods can be grilled has allowed Etxebarri to refine its grill-house menu. This obsession to improve day after day, to purify his creations even more, is still perfectly valid today. The search for absolute refinement is the restaurant's hallmark.

In fact, one of Etxebarri's best-kept secrets is that there is a lot more cuisine involved that can be seen or sensed. This, however, becomes obvious when you discover that many of the foods that are grilled are finished off with emulsions. To make them, they use the pan juices that are released onto the tray where the main ingredient – straight off the grill – is handled before being plated, as right there is the essence of its flavour. These residual liquids are emulsified with others: from stocks, thick stocks and reductions, to sauces, fried oils and vinaigrettes, all rigorously prepared on the spot to provide an additional touch of elegance. The aim: to enhance the flavour and juiciness of the main ingredient and round off the recipe. An extraordinary symbiosis.

This is a very special concept applied at Etxebarri that, however, makes all the difference. Firstly, because for a restaurant with more conventional culinary offerings it is not necessary to finish a recipe with an emulsion. The oil used to sauté, or the sauce of a stew give enough succulence to the dish. However, for the technique of grilling it is almost something demanded by the script as the ingredients that are grilled welcome the additional hydration and juiciness offered by the emulsions. During the first years, Bittor served the food straight

CONTINUES »

'Bittor takes control
of fire. Close at hand,
and to the side of the six
grills are the tools he uses
to tame the wood coals.
Perforated pans, grills
that are less or more open,
'besuguera' grilling baskets
and various pots'

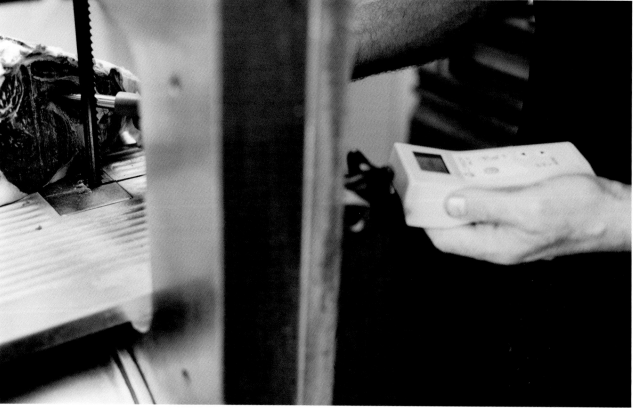

off the grill, but he evolved the recipes until he achieved a perfect combination of unbeatable produce, cooked to perfection and with a touch of the kitchen.

Also exclusive to Etxebarri is the outstanding effort made in the kitchen so that these emulsions can provide that magical touch. Ham bones are blanched three times and are cooked for three hours to obtain a gelatinous stock with a very pronounced flavour, a teaspoonful of which is drizzled over each artichoke. The chicken stock takes 24 hours to cook at 85°C. Red peppers are caramelised for five hours to obtain a syrup that adds shine and flavour to peppers. For the sea bream, garlic and chillies are fried in oil that is emulsified with rhubarb water that is more subtle than vinegar; lemon is used for grouper; and Txakoli for turbot. Oysters, on the other hand, are drizzled with an emulsion made with their own water and emulsified with Iberico pork jowl. And so on for dish after dish.

There is much more to Etxebarri than just produce and wood coals as attested to by the saucepans which, between the dishes of the day and those that are part of the daily routines, steam away on a stove in the kitchen, waiting to be tested. Innovation is in the hands of four cooks: Eneko, Tetsuro, Héctor and Estela. All are trusted completely by Bittor. He places no obstacles in their way and gives them total freedom to buy and try out whatever they want, but he does reserve the right to test them. It is a demanding selection process as only one of every ten creations makes it to the menu. But the freedom to come and go, not at all common in restaurants, endows what Etxebarri offers with fabulous dynamism. The four cooks talk and work together as a team every day.

Eneko Díaz is like a root; a cook who anchors innovation to the land and the farm, to local Basque gastronomy. His origins and knowledge of the world of the farmhouse is what binds him to Bittor: they speak the same language and he is thus the perfect interlocutor for him. Tetsuro Maeda, from Japan, embodies respect for produce. He brings details from the dishes, techniques and logic of Japanese cuisine to what Etxebarri offers. Héctor Gran contributes a touch of innovation, technique and creativity, and is Bittor's right-hand man for the more gastronomic side of things. Estela Izquierdo is the most multi-faceted: from logistics to the perfect handling of fish, as well as the person most trusted by Bittor at the grill.

This devotion to perfection comes from exhaustive knowledge about the produce and its subsequent treatment is another differentiating element. An example of this is the Batavia variety of lettuce. Full of flavour and typical of the Basque Country, it is served with beef chops. Thanks to a perfect understanding of the properties of this lettuce and exactly how to treat it, Tetsuro has managed to make this crunchy morsel a moment of great pleasure. In the vegetable garden, the life of this lettuce must not be compromised. It is picked on summer days when the sun comes up but before it gets hot. In winter it is the other way round because at times it can freeze but, if it has a root, it recovers when it thaws. Thus, one has to wait for it to thaw before cutting and picking it.

Batavia lettuce has a relatively short shelf life and starts oxidizing as soon as the leaves are removed. As it is so delicate, they touch it as little as possible and don't mix it with their hand but with chopsticks to avoid damaging it. Tetsuro puts it in water that is at 8°C, shakes the leaves one by one to remove the water and arranges them on a tray that is put in the fridge. For it to retain its crispiness, the lettuce cannot be wet, but it should not be totally dry either so that it does not lose the level of moisture they want. In the fridge it stays nice and cold, and damp cloths over it keeps in the moisture.

As for the dressing, at Etxebarri they have experimented over 50 times with regard to the ingredients used, as well as quantities and in what order. They seek the perfect balance between salt, olive oil and chacolí vinegar; the latter imparts a very clean acidity, even though only a little is needed. Salt is the most important part of the dressing and so less vinegar and more salt should be used for the lettuce. The order for the dressing is obvious: first the salt, then the vinegar as the salt dissolves well in it, and finally the oil that lightly masks the flavour of the vinegar and salt. It is whisked very little and once dressed is eaten at once. It is served with beef chops as a counterbalance to the excesses of the meat.

On other occasions, perfection is achieved on the grill. Like the white asparagus from Mendavia or Tudela, unique specimens due to their size, mild bitterness and pronounced flavour. In other places, these asparagus are usually previously cooked or blanched and quickly run over the grill to provide them with a pleasant touch of smokiness. At Etxebarri, however, this double cooking process not only goes against their philosophy but is, moreover, totally unnecessary. Asparagus can be grilled perfectly well if the amount of wood coals, the distance, temperature and cooking time are properly controlled. They may be the same asparagus, but the result on the plate changes completely depending on the cooking method used.

Let's see why. Here is top-quality asparagus: the season is short (April and May) and it has been harvested at dawn so it remains totally white. It is arranged on the grill without being previously peeled as this protects its properties and aroma. The asparagus is then covered with a lid and grilled at a considerable distance for about twenty minutes, depending on how thick it is. After leaving it to rest, it is peeled; then dressed with oil and salt, and St George's mushrooms are sliced over it. The result has an extraordinary taste and texture that culminates in an original and flavoursome dish. Compared to other versions, the difference is monumental. To reach this level of sophistication with just one ingredient, only one act was required: evolving how it could be cooked over the wood coals until it was perfect.

In fact, innovation at Etxebarri is often the path to perfection. Imperial beluga caviar is fantastic cold and straight from the tin. Yet Bittor concluded that, after conducting the right experiments, even produce as sublime as this can be improved by grilling. By releasing a little of its oil, its nuances are highlighted and its flavour enhanced. And so innovation, aside from warming the caviar and infusing it with the aroma of apple wood, was based on designing a utensil that would allow the caviar to be grilled but without drying out the eggs. He thus came up with a pan with a double mesh that would allow the seaweed in the lower section to be in contact with the heat and so steam the caviar placed in the upper part.

Other times, innovation is more to do with streamlining the restaurant's own concept, taking advantage of the fact that, having reached the summit, Etxebarri has carte blanche to do as it pleases. Macerating the vegetables from the vegetable garden is a good example. Courgettes, pumpkins, carrots, broccoli and other summer vegetables are perfect for macerating in tomato water – that offers a touch of acidity – for five hours. The particularity is that the previously chopped vegetables are vacuum sealed in a bag so the pressure removes all the air from them; they then soak up all the tomato water as soon as they are put under pressure again. They are served dressed with olive oil and have an extraordinary flavour and texture.

The way they marinate red mullet also breaks with tradition, and is the only fish at Etxebarri that is dehydrated and left to age. It is a short ageing process, just overnight, because the benefits of this resting time cannot be justified at the expense of freshness. But a red mullet that has been filleted and boned, to which 10% of its weight in salt has been placed on its flesh, undergoes a slight loss of liquid that enhances the sweetness of this fish. The fillets are then heated to about 35°C over wood coals and plated with herbs from the vegetable garden, as well as a couple of onion rings. Without being a very bold dish, this minimal ageing allows the sweetness of the red mullet to be enhanced and thus balances the flavour trio of acidity, sweetness and saltiness.

In this search for perfection there is also the desire to offer diners the sensations and flavours of the natural surroundings of the restaurant. A new concept is the herb cracker, a recent addition to the tasting menu. While designing the cracker, the idea was to embody in it the landscape of the hills close to

Etxebarri, in other words, a morsel of sensations linked to the terroir, to the herbs, flowers and aromas of the woods. The aim is for the nature of the Anboto to burst in one's mouth and in one's mind. It is a local version of the *gargouillou*, the iconic dish created by Michel Bras, to which the only licence taken was the addition of avocados from Getaria that intermingle with wild flowers and pea leaves, pinweed, nettles and wild strawberries with a glutinous-rice cracker as its base.

In this process of daily improvement, what is unquestionable at Etxebarri is that they do not take shortcuts. This is very clear from the way their desserts are made because Bittor has made natural desserts his emblem: no stabilisers, emulsifiers or exotic ingredients that don't come from the surrounding area, such as pineapples or mangos. It is also vital that the desserts be seasonal and, on the tasting menu – that complements the menu – make sense and are light. Due to that, perhaps the level of surprise of these typical desserts is not as high, but they are made artisanally, in a purely traditional way.

What is extraordinary is that they are made every day for every meal service. In other words, to make the milk ice cream, the milk is first smoked over the wood coals and then reduced over a very low heat so that the lactose caramelises, a process that needs to be watched constantly. When the first diner arrives, the first ice cream is made in the kitchen, in fact, a normal creamy iced dessert made that day with nothing added. It is an effort not made by others due to lack of time and for economic reasons. But at Etxebarri they do it because it has to do with being self-demanding. It is artisanship: it involves a huge effort...and they could make life a lot easier for themselves! But then it wouldn't be Etxebarri.

A TALENT FOR WINE

Agustí Peris is much more than just the sommelier at Etxebarri. Having trained at the wine cellar and dining room of the legendary elBulli, he is a globetrotter who has provided a consulting service for restaurants and individuals for years. A pioneer about this new way of serving wine and managing the dining room that is much less formal and, at the same time, more welcoming and efficient. His presence at Etxebarri is not permanent as he comes and goes, with no ties but with a commitment to improve day after day, always seeking to travel, learn and share with his clients and friends. It is his life philosophy, a free spirit would be the proper description, and a key figure for the management of a high-performing restaurant.

'I had been to Etxebarri as a diner over 40 times, so I can say that neither the restaurant nor Bittor Arginzoniz were new to me. Bittor occasionally went to Barcelona and we would meet up for lunch. He always said that he wanted to do something with wine, change the wine list, etc. He was aware that he had customers who were interested in wine and he wasn't catering to them. After a few years, I went to Axpe to examine the restaurant's wine cellar and try to turn it around. That was in 2011. I went there for three weeks and I'm still here.

'When I went into the wine cellar, I encountered what I expected in a restaurant of this kind: the usual collection of Riojas, Riberas del Duero, etc. typically found in the Basque Country. 95% were reds and by well-known wineries. The rest was a motley selection of whites, bought depending on what was at a good price, a batch of Reisling and Burgundy, and a luxury brand of champagne. So, the idea was to create a wine list with more whites than reds, based on my experience at el Bulli where the cuisine was subtle, filled with details, where the flavours of the sea were very present on the menu.

'We also had to start working on pairing. However, when you work with a tasting menu with so many very different dishes, it's hard to come up with suggestions that everyone will like, and it'll drive you mad. A dish and a specific wine may go together harmoniously, but when there are lots of dishes...forget it! Although it's true that here things are a little simpler because, at the end of the day, everything boils down to a single cooking technique. Grilling sets the trend for you, I believe more in this idea and the iconic ingredients – elvers, prawns, etc. – together with great wines.

'Another important line of work that had to be developed was for the restaurant to approach winemakers and form bonds with wineries out of respect for the product. We now buy 80% of our wines directly from wineries. What I most like is having a personal relationship with winemakers and this has meant constantly visiting wineries and trying vintage after vintage.

'The result of all of this work is reflected on the wine list. We now have 320 wines, half of which are whites. Here in Spain we don't have much more to explore, the wines that interest me are from very small productions. And from abroad, buying as much as we can directly because it's the only way of getting a certain number of *vignerons*, especially from Burgundy.

'When I buy, I don't necessarily think of the food; I do sometimes, but it's not premeditated. What I am sure of is the kind of wines that we don't want here; for example, very aged and markedly mature wines, although I do have to offer a few because our local clientele has its preferences. Moreover, I always have some bottles on the list out of courtesy, and also because some brands are etched in Bittor's memory. That doesn't mean that classic wines don't interest me because they always interest me, but I pay more attention to what young people are doing. There are areas with young people who are on the right track, as in Ribeira Sacra, el Bierzo and the Canary Islands. Those interest me a lot. The patterns of the big brands are very familiar.

'My challenge has been to dovetail this philosophy with the food at Etxebarri. Basically, its all about seafood cooking and whites, but when we talk about young squid, mushrooms or scrambled eggs, that are the dishes that bring a part of the menu to a close, you can be a bit more daring. You can introduce a glass of red wine as a sort of transition to end that sequence of dishes, something more delicate, but you can also open a great bottle ahead of time. You can play with reds to pair with fish dishes depending on how they are prepared, but that doesn't work with seafood.

'The essential idea is that the drink should provide acidity; acidity stimulates the palate and keeps one's appetite going. Bittor designs the 13 dishes on the tasting menu depending on the produce available, but there is always a pattern. One of Bittor's best qualities is order. He has great judgement when it comes to flavours and for one dish to lead to the next, to clean you, he says. And that is what we seek with the wines. That first moment is important, that first contact with the restaurant is crucial: the welcome, a little water, the anchovy, the butter and something to whet your appetite. That first glass of wine is important.

'When it comes to salivation, the best wines are those that are not too rich but that have depth. I think that whites such as Puligny-Montrachet and Chablis are perfect, but a Meursault is too rich, so I'd go for a Puligny for its linearity and because the lees and wood are not so present. Reisling could work with some dishes, but its acidity is nothing like that of a Chablis and, in addition, it's got that aromatic intensity that can be a bit invasive. I would definitely say that a Burgundy or a Chablis would be my first choice for a bottle of white wine. For a first glass, the idea is to offer a Spanish wine, an Albariño or a Ribeira Sacra, but something light.

'As for reds, I think there are some very interesting wines in el Bierzo, just as in Ribera del Duero when the right conditions come together, and from certain producers. I'm talking about projects involving 20,000 to 30,000 bottles at the most. For climate and terroir, Ribera is superb, but not every year is a great one. Because of a personal affinity, I most like working with wines from California as their qualities are very easy to identify. The formula I suggest for a table of four to six people could be: a first glass (a light white that has not aged too much), a bottle of white, another of red, and a glass of dessert wine to finish.

'As for pairings, our suggestion includes four glasses of wine (three whites and a red, as a general rule), a glass of beer, and a glass of dessert wine to finish. The beer is a concession to Bittor's genius as he makes it on-site, and in theory it should be served in a specific order, in the sequence of clam-oyster-prawn. Although to be honest, the aim is not to pair a dish to a set wine. Finding a balance is always a difficult challenge.'

7

Etxebarri's philosophy is reflected on its menu and Bittor's genuine devotion to quality produce. Rather than enjoying a series of flawlessly executed dishes, diners at Etxebarri are offered a succession of different kinds of produce at their gastronomic best. Ingredients from the vegetable garden picked when they are just right, seafood dictated by the calendar, meat that is at its moment of perfection. Quality, size and freshness are hallmarks of the restaurant's culinary offer.

The factor of proximity is a decisive one that contributes to this: produce and livestock from the farm; from the fish markets of the magical Cantabrian coast; from the secrets hidden in the nearby woods. This does not mean that produce from further afield is banned from Etxebarri's menu. Quite the opposite in fact; if the quality of produce is of the highest category, such as the case of prawns from Palamós, then transport logistics are set in place that allow it to be delivered daily in perfect condition where it will have a place in the sun on Etxebarri's menu. Despite this, for this produce to remain on the menu, that top quality must be maintained.

In truth, surroundings and proximity are important to Bittor because they are a guarantee of quality and freshness, in addition to the fact that they give meaning to his gastronomic philosophy. But, if an ingredient deserves it, Bittor is willing to go to the ends of the world, moving heaven and earth, to make it part of his culinary repertoire. Equally important for him is, of course, seasonality: netting fish about to lay their eggs, hunting woodcock, or gathering mushrooms. Sometimes the season is particularly short, barely a few weeks: this is the case for elvers, teardrop peas, anchovies, fresh pochas beans, small squid, green peppers. They are gifts from the gods.

So, as we have seen unique produce and seasonality are two coordinates that always meet on the menu at Etxebarri. A third core element is fire, as all the main dishes are subjected to the wood coals and are infused with its aroma. And the emulsions, sauces or reduced stocks that are part of the recipes of these delicacies – of extraordinary quality and cooked by this contact with the fire – are also infused in the same way. It is an invisible, hidden and secret culinary touch. But it is a vital culinary touch to complete and perfect each creation.

Faithfully setting these dishes before diners means that the menu has to be created every day. It is a menu that is very much marked by the seasons, but also by the quality that each ingredient displays each day. It must also 'make sense'; in other words, it must be a menu with gastronomic suggestions that are linked to the surroundings, to the local nature, to the world of the farmhouses. Purity, seasonality, fire, succulence and surroundings. With these objectives achieved, each kind of produce comes into its own as the main ingredient in little dishes that are celestial morsels. The result of this culminates in the list of produce shown below.

Whether they appear as a dish of the day or are on the tasting menu (that includes about 15 dishes), each and every one of them is a good example of Etxebarri's culinary offering. The most exquisite produce is combined (red prawns, St George's mushrooms, oysters, sea cucumbers, goose-neck barnacles, caviar, salmon, black variegated scallops), with the strictest seasonality (anchovies, teardrop peas, wild mushrooms, March mushrooms, red mullet, tomatoes, woodcock); traditional Basque dishes (peppers, beef chop, salt cod, kidney beans, small squid, sea bream, kokotxas, cheese crème caramel) with the restaurant's hallmark dishes (scrambled eggs, butter, chorizo, fresh cheese, elvers, croquettes, reduced milk ice cream).

The selection of dishes listed below – including the restaurant's most iconic ones – covers the most representative of the past years, despite the fact that almost no recipe has ever been written down. They are, in any case, a combination of recipes and produce that paint a faithful picture of what Etxebarri's cuisine represents as well as its evolution over the past years.

THE RESULT

ON THE MENU TODAY...

BUTTER

FRESH CHEESE

CHORIZO

CROQUETTE

TOMATO

PUMPKIN

SALMON

CRAB

VELVET CRAB

GOOSE-NECK BARNACLES

CLAMS, COCKLES AND WARTY VENUS CLAMS

VARIEGATED SCALLOPS

MUSSELS

OYSTERS

CAVIAR

LANGOUSTINES / LOBSTER

PRAWNS FROM PALAMÓS

SEA CUCUMBER

ELVERS

BABY OCTOPUSES

YOUNG SQUID

PEPPERS

WILD MUSHROOMS AND AUBERGINES

MARCH MUSHROOMS

ST GEORGE'S MUSHROOMS

EGGS

ARTICHOKES

TEARDROP PEAS

ANCHOVIES

KOKOTXAS

RED MULLET

BONITO

GROUPER

SALT COD

SEA BREAM

WOODCOCK

BEEF CHOP

KID

DESSERTS

MILK ICE CREAM

CHEESE CRÈME CARAMEL

JUNKET

MADELEINES

COCOA SHOT

'Food is sacred and should be treated with humility, respect and honesty. That's what I was taught at home', he repeats often

CHORIZO

thus comes from the best acorn-fed Iberian pigs from Joselito. And the cuts he chooses for his chorizo are the best ones: 'presa' pork shoulder and meat from the 'secreto' cut.

Gastronomically speaking, they are the most extraordinary parts of the animal. The 'presa' is found between the top of the loin and the foreleg, and the main characteristic of this meat is its subtleness. The best thing about the 'secreto', located behind the shoulder and under the belly fat, is its gorgeous marbling. The combination of the two results in juicy, flavoursome meat that melts in the mouth like butter. The elegance of these meats,

combined with the marinade of choricero peppers from Bittor's vegetable garden and a painstaking artisanal process, give rise to this sublime charcuterie. A gift for the palate that at Etxebarri is offered as an amuse-gueule at the start of the tasting menu.

'There is no mystery behind a delicious chorizo. It depends on the breed of the animal, on what it has eaten, which cut is chosen, and the ingredients that go into the marinade. At Etxebarri you can eat a kilo of chorizo and you'll digest it easily. It's simple: you can fool the palate but not the stomach,' Bittor states as proof of quality. But achieving such a high level of excellence requires a good dose of patience. The artisanal process lasts for three days and involves the entire kitchen staff. In two months the chorizo for the whole year is made. There is no room for error.

The adrenaline begins to flow when the 1,000 kilos of meat arrives in four batches, sent from Joselito each winter, just after the slaughter. The recently slaughtered meat is transported at a low temperature to avoid it falling apart and becoming an unusable mass. It must, therefore, be minced immediately, mixing equal quantities of 'presa' and 'secreto'. This minced meat is then marinated for 24 hours with a paste of choricero peppers, water and puréed garlic. By then, the choricero peppers from Bittor's vegetable garden – planted in March, picked in October, and dried during the autumn – should be perfectly dehydrated.

It is also an exercise in artisanship. Each pepper is threaded by its stem, one by one, then plaited together in the same way that garlic and onions are tied. The strings are then hung up in a well-ventilated place (away from the sun) to avoid them going mouldy. Bittor hangs the peppers in the drying shed of his farmhouse where they should remain for

three months to dry out completely. If the weather is too damp, he builds a small fire in the hearth to help the drying process.

After being rehydrated and the pulp extracted, and the marinating has been done, the most delicate phase of making the chorizo begins: stuffing the casing. Bittor does this himself because no one has more experience than him in using the sausage stuffer to fill the pork casings completely but without them breaking. Any imperfection at this stage would create air bubbles in the casing and lead to holes in the cured chorizo. Or it could be more serious: the meat could oxidize, go rotten and months of work would go down the drain.

Afterwards, the staff work as if on an assembly line in Etxebarri's kitchen to carry, cut, tie and store the sausages that are then taken to Bittor's drying shed for the last part of the curing process. Because of the climate of the Atxondo Valley, curing lasts about a month; it not only needs a good breeze, but also requires cold weather. The worst enemy the chorizo could have during this last part of the curing process is the warm, damp southerly wind, particularly in the first two weeks. It is, therefore, vital to check the weather forecast before embarking on those three days of artisanal work.

CHORIZO CHARCUTERIE

INGREDIENTS

— 500 g Iberico 'presa' pork shoulder
— 500 g Iberico 'secreto' pork
— 250 g pulp from choricero peppers from Guernica
— 200 g fresh pork casing
— 25 cloves garlic
— 50 g Guérande salt
— Mineral water

METHOD

— Make a cut in the choricero peppers and remove all the seeds. Hydrate them in a container of water for 24 hours. Boil to rid them of any bugs and to eliminate any impurities. Drain and remove the peppers. Next, using a machine or a sharp knife, separate the pulp from the skin and from any remaining seeds. Keep only the paste-like pulp.
— Mince equal amounts of recently slaughtered meat (Iberico 'presa' and 'secreto') in a mincer. In a suitable sized container, put in the meats and the choricero-pepper paste, the puréed garlic, the salt and water. Mix all the ingredients well and leave in the fridge for 24 hours.
— Use a sausage stuffer to stuff the casing, making sure to avoid oxidation by not allowing air bubbles to form inside. Cut into 25-cm-long sausages and with a width to suit your local curing conditions. Tie a knot at each end.
— Leave to cure in a drying shed where these is a cold breeze for as long as required, depending on the climatic conditions and the desired flavour. When cured, vacuum pack and store in the fridge.
— Cut into slices, place in a small bread

roll and serve. The freshly-made bread should be nice and warm so that the chorizo sweats a little.

CHISTORRA SAUSAGE

— When the marinating has finished, place in rectangular stainless steel moulds to make ingots. Leave in the fridge for 24 hours for the meat to firm up.
— Place in a narrow grilling basket. Roast at a medium height over a medium fire of wood coals for 8 minutes on one side and 4 minutes on the other.
— Serve on a 'talo' or flatbread made from dried corn.

EGG YOLK WITH CHORIZO STOCK

— Make a chorizo stock by cooking slices of chorizo in water. Strain, leave to cool and remove the layer of fat.
— Thicken the stock with potato starch to make it creamy in texture.
— Heat, and add a little fat.
— Confit the egg yolks at 65°C for 10 minutes.
— Ladle two tablespoonfuls of the stock into a bowl and add the egg yolks. Slice St George's mushrooms over the egg yolks and serve.

This recipe has two secrets. On the one hand, at Etxebarri they use their own chickens that are slaughtered that same day and cooked at low temperature for 24 hours in the milk that will be used to make the béchamel sauce. The quality of the chicken's meat comes from the fact that they are fed corn and barley, and roam practically free. In addition, thanks to the slow cooking, the meat remains moist and does not dry out.

On the other hand, having been previously coated in olive oil, the croquette fries on the grill over the wood coals. This results in a fried texture but without the greasiness associated with traditional frying. Furthermore, having been exposed to the wood coals, it absorbs the aroma of the wood. It is fried in a titanium grilling basket invented by Bittor who chose the material as the croquette does not stick to it.

With all this in mind, Bittor developed a traditional recipe to achieve his own, more sophisticated, gastronomic version, not to mention the fact that he uses the best raw materials possible, is very patient when it comes to making them, just as he is with his technique of frying over wood coals that gives the recipe a touch of magic.

CROQUETTE

CROQUETTE OVER WOOD COALS

INGREDIENTS

— 2 chickens
— 1 litre milk
— 150 g butter
— 200 g flour
— 100 ml olive oil
— 200 g breadcrumbs
— Salt

METHOD

— Clean the chickens, cut into quarters and set aside.

— Put the chickens into a large saucepan with the milk and simmer for 24 hours so that the meat remains tender and the milk is infused with the flavour of the chicken.

— Remove the chickens, separate into pieces and finely chop. Set the chicken and the milk aside.

— To make the béchamel, melt the butter in a saucepan. Mix in the flour and stir until totally absorbed. Cook it a little and add the milk.

— Put in the chicken and stir until smooth and creamy.

— Season with salt, set aside and allow to cool.

— Shape the croquette, coat with the breadcrumbs and spray with olive oil. Immediately place it on the grill, right over the wood coals, at a medium height over lively coals so that it fries as it cooks.

The tomatoes at Etxebarri come from Bittor's farmhouse vegetable garden. These local tomatoes can be distinguished by their fine skin, robust flavour and meatiness; their flesh is firm and there are no cavernous holes inside. In addition, if they have been exposed to the sun, they are very sweet, something that makes their quality vary depending on the season, the weather, and the amount of sun.

Bittor is a staunch critic of tomatoes grown in greenhouses. Growing them in the open air of the vegetable garden guarantees quality, but it shortens the season to barely two months: September and October. Their cultivation is rather hit-or-miss as not only does it depend on the sun, but the tomatoes also need the earth to be warm. If it is cold and rainy, the harvest will be affected.

The mild climate of Atxondo offers the ideal conditions for growing tomatoes. Moreover, being just a few metres from the restaurant is a double guarantee of quality: on the one hand, it allows the fruit to be picked when it is perfectly ripe; and, on the other, because no refrigeration is used, no quality of flavour is lost.

The tomatoes at Etxebarri thus have all the properties of organic farming and with no distances or transportation involved. They are eaten whole, peeled and marinated, and quickly run over the wood coals.

TOMATO

MARINATED TOMATO

INGREDIENTS

— Tomato

METHOD

— Scald the tomato in the flames of the wood coals for 15 seconds or until the skin is burned. This will make peeling it easier and will infuse it with the subtle aroma of the wood coals.

— Peel the tomato and then leave it to marinate in oil and salt for a couple of hours. Serve whole.

The pumpkins that Bittor grows in his vegetable garden are elongated, green on the outside and dark orange inside. They are prized for the consistency of their flesh, for their lack of acidity, and for their sweetness and mildness. They are harvested from July to November. Although it is not a vegetable commonly used in Basque cooking, its treatment over wood coals at Etxebarri allows the range of appetizers to be more varied. The roasted rectangles are served with an almond and aromatic herb praline.

The rectangles are roasted at the entrance of the oven, on the wood coals and in direct contact with them; they are thus immediately penetrated by the heat and cook at once. The idea is for the pumpkin to soften and become tender as quickly as possible, and not to dry out or burn. The rectangles are in direct contact with the wood coals that are not as incandescent as those of the grill, allowing the pumpkin to roast but not burn. The temperature is very high and there is also less oxygen as the oven is closed.

For the praline, the almonds are blanched and chopped, then butter is added and the two are beaten to a sandy texture. The praline is topped with grated lemon zest and a few bold-flavoured leaves and flowers such as nasturtium whose hints of wasabi and horseradish enhance the dish. The sweetness and tenderness of the roasted pumpkin are heightened by the stronger flavour of the aromatic leaves, while the praline acts as a link between the two.

PUMPKIN

PUMPKIN STICK WITH ALMOND PRALINE

INGREDIENTS

— 150 g pumpkin per rectangle

— 75 g dry-roasted almonds

— 1 tsp butter

— Grated zest of 1 lemon

— A few nasturtium leaves

METHOD

— Peel the fresh pumpkin and cut into rectangles.

— Place them at the entrance of the oven, on the wood coals, for 1 - 2 minutes at the most, just on one side.

— Remove the rectangles and spread the almond praline on the upper side as if it were butter

— Grate the lemon zest. Decorate the rectangle with grated lemon zest and nasturtium leaves.

A delicious smoked dish for spring that is only on the menu at Etxebarri depending on the size, quality and availability of the salmon each season. In addition to being a good size and fatty, they must have been caught in the waters of wild-salmon rivers in Asturias and Cantabria where they swim upstream every spring. This endows their flesh with great flavour and succulence. The season extends to the beginning of July.

The marinade – with grated orange and lemon zest, and fennel – gives a touch of sweetness without the need for sugar. The smoking process is instant, barely the time required to take the plate to the table, and is done by presenting it in a lidded wooden box containing a small smoker. This device is a little beaker containing a burning wood coal, dried lemon peel and chamomile. It is wonderfully aromatic and not very bitter. The recipe thus achieves a perfect combination of wood and aroma.

SALMON

SMOKED SALMON

INGREDIENTS

— Fresh salmon from the River Sella

— Grated lemon zest

— Grated orange zest

— Fennel

— Salt

— Dried lemon peel

— Chamomile

METHOD

— Gut and clean the salmon and separate the two fillets. Marinate them in the orange and lemon zests, the fennel and salt for 1 hour and 30 minutes. Next, clean them and set them aside in olive oil for 2 - 3 hours.

— Slice the fillets as you would for sashimi and place them in a wooden box with the smoker, in which is a burning wood coal, dried lemon peel and chamomile. Put the lid on the box and serve just seconds after the salmon has become infused with the aromas of the wood coal and the citrus zests.

Crabs have a structure that is different from other marine creatures. Their hard outer shell means that their delicate flesh cooks in their own juices, without contact with water or oil. This dish is composed of a small cone filled with crabmeat, made with the flesh of crabs from the Cantabrian Sea that are supplied by Laureano Oubiña in Galicia. The crabs must be big so they can be roasted over the grill with no risk of them drying out inside; this requires extreme mastery and technique in managing the wood coals. This particular difficulty has, in fact, been why this crustacean has traditionally been kept far from the grill.

Both males and females are used, and the roe of the latter serves to prepare a cream sauce. The cone is made from an infusion of kombu seaweed mixed with potato starch. The resulting dough is grilled over the wood coals (instead of being fried) to make it crispy.

Another version of this dish is made with sea urchins The starch is mixed with water as sea urchins eat seaweed. It is served with a little pumpkin cream. In both cases, the combination of flavours is extraordinary.

CRAB

INGREDIENTS

— 1 male or female crab from the Cantabrian Sea

— Oil

— Potato starch

— Kombu seaweed stock

— Fennel fronds

METHOD

— Place the crabs directly on the grill, covered with a lid, underside facing upwards and over a lively fire for 10 - 15 minutes until the shell comes away easily.

— When they are done, remove the legs, crack them open, shred the meat and set aside any liquid they release.

— Using the legs and shell, prepare an oil and add a touch of toasted shell. Mix the oil with the crabmeat.

— Use the coral to make a cream sauce as you would a Hollandaise, but substituting the egg yolks with the roe. Do this carefully as at 70°C it begins to thicken. When you have the desired consistency, add a splash of sherry or Manzanilla to the cream sauce.

— To make the cone, infuse the kombu seaweed in cold water, leaving it overnight in the water with potato starch. Cook until creamy in consistency; spread this cream onto a tray and dehydrate. Cut and then shape the cones over the grill. Set the grill at a height where the temperature is 150°C.

— When ready to serve, fill the cones with the cream sauce and the crabmeat that has been lightly sautéed over the wood coals. Top with a fennel frond.

Caught in the cold, rough waters of the Cantabrian Sea and served between November and May, at Etxebarri they are fresh and flavoursome, and weigh 250 grams each. Magnificent creatures that are trapped in crab pots, they are taken to the port of Santoña and end up in the restaurant's tank. From there to the grill so that they are infused with the aroma of the wood coals. The reason they are so good is due to their quality, size, where they come from and their seasonality, but the secret of their gastronomic appeal is achieved on the grill thanks to talent and a clinical eye.

They are cooked somewhat differently; not straight on the grill but in a mesh pan. But they are not sautéed: they are grilled. And that is where the difficulty lies, because velvet crabs dry out very easily. To prevent this, they are placed in the pan and covered with a lid. Initially, they are placed right-side up to numb them and then they are immediately turned over so that they do not lose any liquid; this stops the crabs from turning over and breaking their claws as they try to do so.

By covering them, the inside of the crabs cook at an even temperature, cooking gently in their own juices and without salt or oil. You can tell when they are done because the liquid inside the shell and towards the back begins boiling and bubbling. These are signs that it is cooked to perfection. The magic of this recipe lies in the pronounced taste of seafood these crabs have: notes that are briny and sweet, coupled with the distinctly aromatic touch of the wood coals. As with almost all crustaceans, the females are better tasting than the males.

VELVET CRABS OVER WOOD COALS

INGREDIENTS

— 1 - 2 velvet crabs weighing 250 g each

METHOD

— Place the velvet crabs right-side up in a mesh pan and place over the wood coals at a medium height. Cover with a lid.

— After a few seconds, turn them over so that they are upside down. Grill for 5 minutes over hot wood coals or until the liquid in them begins bubbling. Remove from the pan.

— Open the shell, use a knife to cut out the cartilage and gills, cut in half and serve.

The coldness of the water, the salinity and the density of the sea along the Costa de la Muerte (Coast of Death) are why this Galician crustacean is considered to be the king of the sea. Their unmistakable flavour, like a sip of the ocean, is combined with the way they are gathered – the stuff of legend – from cliffs battered by the sea breaking violently against them, and where the *percebeiros* who gather them risk their lives.

Aside from coming from Galicia, it is important that they are the right size. The perfect goose-neck barnacle is short and stout, almost as wide as it is high, regardless of how long it is. They are delivered live to Etxebarri and are kept for up to three days in a cloth soaked in seawater.

Bittor invented a special container to cook them over wood coals and not, as it the culinary norm, in boiling water. This utensil allows the goose-neck barnacles to be cooked differently, as at Etxebarri they are not boiled but steamed over the wood coals. They are sprayed with seawater so they steam in their own juices and, furthermore, they are infused with the aroma of the wood coals. No salt – or any other condiment – is added.

The container is covered while the barnacles cook and is also used to serve them at the table.

GOOSE-NECK BARNACLES

INGREDIENTS

— 100 g Galician goose-neck barnacles (the amount for a tasting menu)

— 1 litre seawater

METHOD

— Place the goose-neck barnacles in the container, spray with seawater and put the container onto the main grill, quite close to the fire.

— Cover the container with a lid and grill over the very hot wood coals for 5 minutes.

— Remove and serve the barnacles in the same container.

Three other bivalve molluscs from the Costa de la Muerte – aside from variegated scallops – are served at Etxebarri. Clams, cockles and warty venus clams are cooked over wood coals in the same way: they are placed on the main grill just until they open; they are then removed so that no liquid is lost. As with other extraordinarily good Galician seafood, they require no more cooking than the perfect cooking time. Their gastronomic qualities carry the seal of the Costa de la Muerte.

The cold sea and, above all, the strong currents that oxygenate and bring nutrients to these waters are what constitute the creation of this unique marine biodiversity. This plays a vital role in the extraordinary quality of the seafood here; it needs almost no culinary treatment for its properties and subtleness to come through. Most importantly, its natural flavour must be preserved.

The delicate texture and intense taste of the sea are what make the clams and cockles outstanding. With meat that has a more pronounced flavour and a more intense aroma of the sea, warty venus clams are a little known Galician seafood. Etxebarri's selection criterion demands all three molluscs to be the maximum size so that they are suitable for grilling over wood coals. Large, top-quality ones are always necessary requirements.

They are grilled straight over lively wood coals at a medium height. They are removed from the fire as soon as they open, unlike for variegated scallops, and are placed on a tray. A light garlic and oil emulsion – made with the juices that remain on the tray, plus a touch of acidity provided by a drop of lemon – is poured over the molluscs.

CLAMS, COCKLES AND WARTY VENUS CLAMS OVER WOOD COALS

INGREDIENTS

— 12 Palourde clams, cockles or warty venus clams, XXL size

— 1 lemon

— 1 tbsp olive oil

— Garlic and chilli

METHOD

— Place the molluscs straight on the main grill, over lively wood coals at a medium height. Remove them when they open and place on a serving plate so their liquid is not lost.

— Emulsify hot oil and garlic, the liquid from the molluscs and a few drops of lemon juice; pour a teaspoonful over each mollusc. Serve.

Only the black variegated scallop is served at Etxebarri. It is a rare, winter mollusc that has a short season. What makes this iconic Galician shellfish unique is that it has a much brinier flavour than its sister's, the white variegated scallop, as well as a fattier texture. It is considered to be one of the most exceptional delicacies found in the coastal waters of Galicia.

Just as with the clams, the goal is not to dehydrate them over the wood coals or allow them to lose their liquid; but, unlike with the clams, these are not removed from the fire as soon as they open, but are left a little longer until cooked to perfection. The unusual technique used at Etxebarri is that the scallop meat – attached to the upper shell – is steamed thanks to the water and juices in the lower shell.

This steam is infused with the aroma of the wood coals so that it completes the cooking process and results in variegated scallops that melt like butter in the mouth. After plating, and to highlight the dish, a light sea-urchin emulsion that adds an extra flavour is poured over them.

VARIEGATED SCALLOPS

BLACK VARIEGATED SCALLOPS OVER WOOD COALS WITH SEA-URCHIN JUS

INGREDIENTS

— 12 black variegated scallops
— 1 sea urchin per serving
— Garlic, chilli and olive oil

METHOD

— Open the sea urchins, remove the flesh and set aside in a container. Strain the seawater and the sea urchin liquid into another bowl, and set aside.

— Blend the sea-urchin coral and cook in a saucepan with a little water. Gently simmer this paste, gradually adding the seawater and sea-urchin liquid until the mixture is creamy in consistency. Remove from the heat and set aside.

— Place the variegated scallops onto the grill. Grill at a medium height over lively wood coals until they open. Leave on the grill for 2 more minutes, then remove.

— Cut the meat from the shell to make it easier to eat them. Pour a little of the garlic and oil sauce (macerated with the chilli) over each scallop. Also pour a teaspoonful of the sea-urchin jus over each one.

The mussels served at Etxebarri come from Mont Saint-Michel in Normandy and enjoy a designation of origin. Their characteristics are similar to Galician mussels. They are larger than rock mussels, are bright orange and have a pronounced flavour. Their flesh is silky and springy and is very elegant on the palate. They are at their best from July to October.

There are two main key elements to this recipe: they are steamed in their own juices and they absorb the fragrance of the wood coals. This leads to succulent, aromatic mussels. To do this, Bittor had to invent a specific utensil that would prevent the loss of liquids yet, at the same time, allow the aroma of the wood coals to enter. At first, he put the mussels on the grill as he did with the clams, but the mussels lost their liquid. With nothing to guide him, he came up with a container with a volcano-shaped base through which the aroma could enter, while the liquid became the steam that would cook the mussels.

The pot has a glass lid via which you can see exactly when the mussels begin to open so they can be removed from the fire, removed from their shells and served. A few drops of a strained emulsion made with the mussels' cooking liquid combined with carrot juice are added to the dish. The carotene enhances the sweetness of the mussels.

MUSSELS

STEAMED MUSSELS WITH CARROT JUICE

INGREDIENTS

— 200 g Normandy mussels from the south of Mont Saint-Michel

— 4 carrots (for the carrot juice)

METHOD

— Use a knife to scrape the mussel shells one by one and set aside.

— Put the mussels in a covered pot and place over lively wood coals so they steam in their own liquid.

— Remove the mussels as soon as they open, shell them and serve on a serving plate.

— Blend the liquid from the mussels with the carrot juice and strain. Pour a spoonful of the liquid over each mussel and serve.

When grilling oysters, it is important to use large ones. The heat shrinks small ones and they lose their firmness. Bittor thus chooses to use the excellent Gillardeau oysters (number o) that are particularly suited to being grilled thanks to their meatiness and juiciness. Furthermore, these oysters from Brittany are very characteristic and offer a superb balance of intense flavour and delicateness, sweetness and brininess.

To be exact, their pronounced brininess combines perfectly with the light aroma of the oak wood coals. The creamy texture of the Gillardeau oysters merges with this flavour and aroma, as do their freshness and their juice that is like a hint of the sea. They are topped with an emulsion of Joselito Iberico pork jowl that adds an element of silkiness. The season lasts all year, although oysters are at their best during the winter months.

OYSTERS OVER WOOD COALS

INGREDIENTS

— 2 Gillardeau oysters (number o)
— 15 g Joselito Iberico pork jowl
— 1 tbsp borage juice
— Spinach leaves or seaweed

METHOD

— Shuck the oysters and remove from the shells. Set the shells and the water they contain aside. Use scissors to cut away the beards around the flesh and discard as they have a bitter taste.

— Finely slice the pork jowl and melt it in a little saucepan over a low heat so that it renders its fat. Set aside.

— Pour the water from the shells over the two oysters and place them on a narrow grilling basket. Set aside.

— Arrange wood coals that give off a gentle heat under the grill and place the grilling basket 10 centimetres above them. Grill for a maximum of 1 minute each side, constantly spraying them with liquid as they cook. Remove.

— Arrange a bed of blanched spinach leaves in each shell and place an oyster in each one. You can substitute the spinach with seaweed.

— Blend some of the liquid from the oysters with the borage juice and a teaspoonful of the pork-jowl fat. Brush the oysters with the emulsion and serve.

One of the most appreciated delicacies thanks to its complex, subtle and lingering flavour, at Etxebarri it has a brief encounter with the wood coals that enhance its virtues. To do so, Bittor had to invent a specific utensil; a pan with holes in the bottom and two meshes inside it, plus a lid. A handful of damp seaweed is placed on the lower mesh, almost touching the wood coals.

As it heats up, the seaweed steams the eggs that are placed on the upper mesh, preventing them from drying out. The pan is covered with a lid and left over a very low fire for ten minutes.

The caviar he uses is Iranian imperial beluga; it is perfect because the eggs are mild yet large, about three millimetres. For Bittor it is vital that the caviar has been extracted as recently as possible so that its freshness stands out, and also that it is as natural as possible, in other words, has a minimal amount of salt. Due to caviar's characteristics, salt is a necessary preservative, but too much can ruin the delicateness, complexity and subtlety of these sturgeon eggs.

Over the wood coals, the caviar is infused with the aroma of apple wood coals, while exposure to the heat makes the eggs a little less oily. The silky texture is thus maintained and its complex and lingering flavour is enhanced.

The temperature of the wood coals is low, about 50°C, and the warmth endows the caviar with nuances that are not appreciated when cold. It is eaten in one mouthful on a crispy almond biscuit.

CAVIAR

CAVIAR

INGREDIENTS

— 15 - 20 g imperial beluga caviar (per serving)

— 50 g seaweed such as wakame

— 1 piece apple wood firewood

— 1 tbsp almond paste

METHOD

— Work the almond paste and shape it like a tuile, leaving it to dry at 70°C for 6 hours over a cylinder. Set aside.

— In the caviar pan, place the seaweed on the lower mesh and the caviar on the upper mesh. Place on the grill, very close to the wood coals and leave to steam over a low fire for 10 minutes.

— Place the warm caviar in the tuile and serve.

The langoustines at Etxebarri come exclusively from the Bermeo coast. These crustaceans could not come from any other port as they are very delicate, only staying alive if just caught and kept in proper conditions. The fishermen phone Bittor when their catch is of the size he wants and, as soon as the langoustines come out of the sea, they are sent to Etxebarri covered in a damp cloth. They survive in the tank at the restaurant in icy water, without food, for two weeks, even more if fed on swordfish. However, if the water is not cold enough, they quickly perish.

Etxebarri requires that they be alive and that they be large. In addition, it is important that they were caught in a traditional way with lobster traps and pots. In this way, unlike trawling, the langoustines come out of the sea alive, unharmed and with no loss of limbs. The best season coincides with the coldest months of the year, from November to January, and is when they are gastronomically at their finest. For many it is the most elegant seafood, embodying the best of the sea and has an intensely briny flavour. The texture of its tail is splendid: the meat is compact and firm as can be appreciated by the little resistance it offers when bitten into, and its slightly sweet flavour closes the virtuous circle.

The lobsters chosen by Bittor come from the Cantabrian Sea or from Scottish waters. It is the lobster par excellence, the species whose juicy and flavoursome meat with an intensely briny taste shows off its gastronomic superiority. They are caught in lobster pots baited with fish, set in rocky areas frequented by these crustaceans. From a gastronomic point of view, the females are more esteemed as they have more coral, the briny taste of which, is particularly delicious.

Both lobsters and langoustines require minimal culinary treatment. They are grilled in their own juices and require no condiment. They are not sprayed with oil, seasoned with salt or even accompanied by an emulsion. The secret lies in freshness, size and being cooked to perfection.

LANGOUSTINES AND LOBSTER OVER WOOD COALS

INGREDIENTS

— Live langoustines from the Cantabrian Sea weighing 400 g each

— 1 lobster from the Cantabrian Sea weighing 1 kg

METHOD

— Cut the langoustines in half lengthways while still alive and remove the intestines from the tails. Do the same with the lobster.

— Place the langoustines and the lobster – cut side up – on the grill, almost touching the wood coals that should be lively embers but half consumed. There should be more wood coals below the heads and claws, and less under the tails where the heat should be lower.

— Grill the langoustines for 10 minutes on one side only, and then remove.

— Do the same with the lobster, but for 15 minutes. There should be more wood coals under the claws so that they grill at the same rate as the rest of the body.

— Remove the langoustines and the lobster, give the claws a bash with a mallet and serve.

There are three core pillars behind the excellence of the red prawns served at Etxebarri. One of them is the raw material. These prawns weigh 60 g each and have fabulously firm meat as a result of the exceptional properties of the habitat in which they live: two small fishing grounds in the waters of Palamós that are little-known places and where the prawns are caught quickly and responsibly so they are not injured in the net. They could not be fresher as the prawns caught that day are sent off to Etxebarri that same afternoon.

The logistics by road from Gerona to Biscay are arranged in such a way that the prawns lose none of their original properties. They travel overnight, partially immersed in isothermal buckets containing seawater and ice. On reaching Etxebarri, the water is immediately changed and the seawater and ice are replaced until the meal service begins. It is essential to conserve them so that the extraordinary texture of the prawns is ensured.

Lastly, the goal when grilling them is to 'cook them so that they are done, yet intact, and look as if they have just been caught,' Bittor explains. The difficulty lies in grilling them so that neither half is too cooked or remains raw. He puts fewer wood coals under the body and livelier wood coals under the heads so that they cook more. According to Bittor, it is crucial to conserve the juices in the prawn's heads as it is 'the best fish soup a cook can offer you'.

PRAWNS FROM PALAMÓS

RED PRAWNS OVER WOOD COALS

INGREDIENTS

— Prawns
— Olive oil

METHOD

— Take the prawns out of the seawater and ice, dry them and set aside. They are served whole and there is no need to remove the antennae, nor to salt them as the seawater provides the perfect point of salinity.

— Arrange two levels of wood coals under the grill. A livelier one, so that the heat reaches the heads and where they join the bodies; and a smaller one to cook the prawn tails to perfection.

— Spray the prawns with olive oil and place on the grill. Grill over a low heat and at a medium height for 3 and 2 minutes per side, respectively. Remove and serve.

Sea cucumbers were perhaps the raw material that gave Bittor the most trouble or, at least, the one that gave him the most work before coming up with his technique and getting the perfect point of doneness on the grill. It is a Mediterranean creature that, at first, Bittor was unfamiliar with and so his instinct was to grill it at a certain height. It didn't work: it cooked but its consistency was like chewing gum. As he subjected the sea cucumbers to higher temperatures and put them closer to the wood coals, the better they became. Until he concluded that the perfect technique lay in placing the sea cucumbers straight onto the live wood coals.

He thus discovered that it was necessary to subject sea cucumbers to high temperatures and hot embers; this broke their fibrous network, leaving them tender yet crunchy at the same time. The combination of meatiness, firmness and a taste of the sea, in addition to their crunchy texture, come together in an extraordinary dish that Etxebarri has elevated to gastronomic excellence. It is not always on the menu because Bittor insists they should be meaty and big. When they are available, they are served with baby broad beans or sautéed white pocha beans.

SEA CUCUMBER

INGREDIENTS

— 4 whole sea cucumbers
from Palamós

— 50 ml olive oil

— 1 small piece hot chilli pepper

— 40 g peeled baby broad beans (accompaniment)

— Salt

METHOD

— Wash the sea cucumbers to remove all the sand. The fishermen wash them as soon as they come out of the water so that at Etxebarri they arrive clean. Cut both ends off the creatures, open them and wash under cold running water.

— Spray the sea cucumbers all over with olive oil, arrange them in a narrow grilling basket and place it straight onto the live wood coals.

— Grill for 1 minute on one side and 30 seconds on the other. Remove, place on a tray, season with salt and top the sea cucumbers with a traditional sauce of hot chilli pepper fried in oil.

— Arrange the sea cucumbers on a bed of baby broad beans or sautéed white pocha beans and pour the remaining liquid from the tray (emulsified with the juices from the sea cucumbers) over the top.

ELVERS

These creatures from the Mediterranean come from a specific fishing ground in Palamós (Gerona) where the sand is coarser than that of others in the area. This is an important factor because one of the difficulties before cooking baby octopuses is to remove all the sand. As this particular sand is coarser, it is easier to clean them after having turned their heads inside out.

This recipe is a true delicacy if the baby octopuses are no longer than 1.5 centimetres: the ideal ones are 1 centimetre long, and need just a quick toss in the pan to sauté them over the wood coals. The result is a baby octopus with a delicate, juicy texture brimming with the taste of the sea.

They are served on a flavoursome bed of confit red onions together with a line of squid-ink sauce alongside them.

BABY OCTOPUSES

BABY OCTOPUSES OVER WOOD COALS

INGREDIENTS

— 100 g baby octopuses 1 - 1.5-cm long

— 4 red onions

— Squid ink

— 100 ml olive oil

— Salt

METHOD

— Clean the baby octopuses inside, one by one, first removing the denticles and then turning their heads inside out to remove all the sand.

— Chop the red onions very finely and confit them at a low temperature for an hour until they caramelise. Set aside.

— For the ink sauce, sweat the red onion, combine it with the squid ink, blend and strain through a conical strainer. Set aside.

— Spray the baby octopuses with olive oil and sauté in a mesh pan over a lively fire and close to the wood coals.

— Remove and plate the baby octopuses on the bed of confit red onion and paint the dish with the squid-ink sauce.

This is another classic ingredient of Basque cuisine and served at Etxebarri from the end of July to September when they are the perfect size for grilling: from 8 to 10 centimetres long. It is important that the squid have not grown too much as their texture hardens as they become bigger. When they are medium sized their texture is still delicate and their flavour excellent.

Jig-caught squid are a delicacy, but the season is short and they are not easy to catch as they are fished artisanally. However, this technique is vital from a gastronomic standpoint: by catching them one by one they are not dragged, they have not flapped around or become injured in a net, nor do they contain sand; their original texture thus remains intact. Furthermore, this technique is meant to fool the squid so that they do not feel attacked as they are caught and not release their ink to defend themselves.

At Etxebarri they come from Santoña and are run over the grill very quickly, but at a high temperature. They are served on a bed of confit onions and the plate is painted with a traditional squid-ink sauce.

YOUNG SQUID OVER WOOD COALS

INGREDIENTS

— 4 medium-sized jig-caught squid (per serving)

— 4 red onions

— 100 ml olive oil

— Salt

METHOD

— To clean the squid, carefully remove the heads, remove the innards and the pen very gently to avoid breaking the ink sacs. Put the head with its tentacles back and set the ink aside.

— Chop the red onions very finely and confit them at a low temperature for an hour until they caramelise. Set aside.

— For the ink sauce, sweat the red onion, combine it with the squid ink, blend and strain through a conical strainer. Set aside.

— Spray the squid with olive oil, and arrange them in a narrow grilling basket close to the live wood coals. Grill over a lively fire for a minute on each side. Season with salt and remove from the heat.

— Plate the squid on a bed of confit red onion and paint the dish with the squid-ink sauce.

Peppers are, regardless of the variety, originally from America. It was Christopher Columbus who, following his second expedition to the new continent in 1493, introduced this vegetable and its seeds to Spain. From there, its cultivation expanded to France, Italy and the rest of Europe where it was widely accepted as a complement to black pepper, the most popular spice of the day. The Spanish and Portuguese spread the use of peppers eastwards; first to the Philippines and then to the rest of Asia where it was absorbed into the local cuisines.

There are many varieties of the species *Capsicum annuum* and they are grown and eaten all over the world. They are classified into two general groups: hot and sweet. It was not until the 20th century – when varieties began to be distinguished from each other and selected – that the larger, fleshier and sweeter varieties were grown, although this selection of sweeter peppers had already been carried out by Spanish priests on their return from America. When peppers are young they are green, mild and narrow, becoming red as they ripen and as their flavour becomes more pronounced and sweeter.

In the Basque Country there is a deep-rooted tradition of eating this vegetable. The most famous are choricero peppers, bell peppers, Guernica peppers, piquillo peppers, cristal peppers, and chilli peppers. Bittor grows two varieties in his vegetable garden: choricero and bell peppers. The former owe their name to the fact that they have always been used on farms to make chorizo; they are dried after having been harvested, and are used to make the marinade for chorizo and chistorra sausages as well as for 'painting' plates.

The latter are served at Etxebarri as a main course – when they are fresh – with seasonal mushrooms. And they are always used to accompany salt cod and to make reductions.

CHORICERO PEPPERS

Depending on the weather, they are sown at the end of winter or at the start of spring as they don't like the cold. After being planted, they give green peppers that are delicate and perfect for frying. As they ripen on the plant, they change colour and go from yellow to red, reaching full ripeness and size from September onwards. The ones that flower first are the most flavoursome and the seeds of these plants are used for planting the following season.

Harvesting begins in October. By then, the skin of the peppers is too thick and frying them is no longer an option, but they are grilled or, more commonly, hung up to dry throughout the autumn. The drying process ends in winter, usually from January onwards and coincides with the pig slaughter. This makes it possible, once they have been hydrated, to use choricero peppers all year long and enjoy this ingredient that is essential to make a Vizcaina sauce and many other Basque recipes. Their hint of bitter-sweetness is appreciated, and they are much more bitter than bell peppers, ñora peppers or paprika.

This recipe calls for just-flowered choricero peppers when they are still green, tender and small. It is important to pick them before they form their skin as this makes their texture tougher; they then lose their delicateness and are no longer good for frying.

This recipe combines the hint of bitterness of the green peppers with the bitter-sweetness of the choricero peppers, in addition to showing off the delicate texture of the peppers with the crispiness of the tempura batter. Frying over wood coals in a modified wok allows the aroma of the wood coals to infuse the peppers with the subtle fragrance of the firewood.

GREEN PEPPERS

GREEN PEPPERS IN TEMPURA BATTER

INGREDIENTS

— Green peppers

METHOD

— Cut the peppers lengthways and fill the cavities with choricero pepper pulp.

— Dredge the peppers in a tempura batter of flour and water and fry them in a wok of very hot oil over wood coals.

— Remove from the heat after 20 seconds and drain on kitchen paper before serving.

BELL PEPPERS

These are harvested from Bittor's vegetable garden from the end of summer until mid autumn, depending on the weather, usually coinciding with September, October and the start of November. They are larger and fleshier than choricero peppers, and are sweeter and juicier. In the kitchen they are used fresh and ripe, in other words, when they are completely red and of a good size.

At Etxebarri they are served grilled regardless of whether they are part of a main course with wild mushrooms, or to accompany salt cod. They are arranged over the direct fire of the wood coals until their skin is charred. They are removed, put into a saucepan and covered with cling film, and left overnight to sweat; this makes peeling them easier. They are peeled the next day; the stalk and seeds are removed, and they are spread on an oven tray. This tray is put into the residual oven that is still hot from the previous day and left to dehydrate for half an hour each side.

Some of them are tinned after having been grilled and cooked au confit. These are the peppers that, when out of season, are served as an accompaniment to grilled salt cod.

This dish of bell peppers is served in season with charcoal burner mushrooms (*urretxas* in Euskera) that are abundant in the Urkiola Nature Reserve and which, because of their delicious flavour, are most appreciated in the Basque Country. These green-capped mushrooms – that mainly grow in beech woods – are found in summer, although the season can last until autumn. After being grilled, the peppers are confit and served with these mushrooms that are sautéed in a mesh pan over wood coals.

CONFIT BELL PEPPERS WITH CHARCOAL BURNER MUSHROOMS

INGREDIENTS

— Bell peppers
— Mushrooms

METHOD

— When they have been grilled, put the peppers into an earthenware pot with olive oil and a touch of garlic and confit for 4 hours in the residual heat of the oven.

— Use a cloth to clean the mushrooms. Sauté them in a mesh pan at a medium height over lively wood coals for 3 minutes.

— Arrange the peppers on a plate, top with the charcoal burner mushrooms and pour over an emulsion made with the cooking oil from the peppers and the juices from the mushrooms.

At Etxebarri they gather three species of porcini or *Boletus.* The visually attractive pine boletes are white inside, have a garnet-coloured cap and brown stem. Their flesh is consistent and firm, and their flavour is milder but more perfumed than that of other wild mushrooms. They appear in July and well into winter. Their season coincides with that of *Boletus edulis,* whose longer stems are darker brown, their caps brown and the underside of the cap is spongy and green. They are mild and sweet in taste. Lastly, *Boletus reticulatus* have dark brown caps that are more compact. They are gathered in July and August.

This variety is very common in the environs of Etxebarri, in particular when it rains a lot and very heavily, or when it hails. They grow in any woods, usually pine, beech and chestnut, as long as the dampness is right for them. Gastronomically, because of their pronounced yet mild aroma and flavour, they are very much esteemed in the Basque Country. At Etxebarri they are paired with grilled aubergines from Bittor's vegetable garden, whose season, from the end of summer to the end of autumn, coincides with that of the wild mushrooms. The meatiness and juiciness of the aubergines mingle with the delicacy and the perfume of the wild mushrooms.

WILD MUSHROOMS AND AUBERGINES

INGREDIENTS

— 2 or 3 wild mushrooms

— 1 small aubergine

— 50 ml sunflower oil for spraying

— 2 leaves each of ground-ivy and yarrow

— Salt

METHOD

— Roast the aubergine in the oven with a lively fire until the skin has charred. Next, and while they are still hot, peel off the skin and keep any liquid the aubergine releases.

— Cut the flesh into dice the same size as those of the mushrooms, and set aside on a tray.

— Clean the mushrooms with a cloth and use a knife to scrape away any black bits.

— Roast the mushroom trimmings in the residual heat of the wood oven. Add a little water and leave to reduce for 3 hours or until sauce-like in texture. Set aside.

— Spray the mushrooms with sunflower oil and place them in the mesh pan. Cover the pan with a lid and grill over the wood coals. Confit over a low heat for 15 minutes, then remove.

— Place the tray of aubergine dice in the oven for 1 minute to warm through and then remove.

— Combine the diced aubergine with the mushrooms on a serving plate, plate and season with salt. Pour a little emulsion made from the mushroom and aubergine juices over the dish. Pour the sauce over the dish and decorate with 2 leaves each of ground-ivy and yarrow.

March mushrooms have black stems and caps, and are white and meaty inside. They grow in January and can be gathered until spring. Their preferred habitat is beech woods, although they can occasionally be found in pine woods. Even though these mushrooms always grow in the same places, they are rare and hard to find. They like the damp, the cold, the snow and, above all, snowmelt.

For Bittor they are different from all the others and it is one of his favourite varieties. He likes their meatiness, their characteristic woody flavour and their touch of bitterness. They are usually used in scrambled eggs, but at Etxebarri they are sautéed over wood coals. When they are gathered, they do not have much aroma, but their intense perfume is released when cooked. The sautéeing technique used is different from that used for St George's mushrooms and requires more time to cook.

The recipe calls for an onion stock whose sweetness and mildness balances the strong woody flavour and the bitterness of the March mushrooms. To enhance the taste of the stock, the onions are sliced and dehydrated for 24 hours. The stock should not be reduced; it is a stock that lightens the dish. The mushrooms are served in a bowl and eaten with a spoon.

MARCH MUSHOOROMS WITH ONION STOCK

INGREDIENTS

— 250 g March mushrooms

— 4 - 5 onions

— 50 ml sunflower oil

— Salt

METHOD

— Slice the onions, arrange on a flat surface and leave to dry for a day at 28 - 30°C, or in a very warm place.

— Clean the mushrooms with a cloth, cut off from the base of the stem and cut into medium-sized pieces.

— Boil the onion slices in water over a medium heat for 1 hour, and then strain. Season very lightly with salt.

— Spray the March mushrooms with sunflower oil and sauté for 5 minutes in a mesh pan at a medium height over lively wood coals.

— Season with salt, remove from the pan and place in a bowl. Pour in a base of the onion stock.

St George's mushrooms are one of the Basque Country's gastronomic treasures. Known locally as *perretxiko* and *ziza,* these spring mushrooms are prized for their delicacy, their flesh and, above all, for their extraordinary aroma that can be smelled from a distance, and is more pronounced if they grow at a higher altitude. Their colours range from white and beige to yellow, and their texture is firm and meaty, yet light. They grow on the slopes of the peaks and all the way to the summit as the weather gets warmer. They like drizzle, damp and mugginess, but not the wind.

Furthermore, it is the most native and abundant of the wild mushrooms in the Atxondo Valley. They arrive at Etxebarri, gathered that same day, and are stored in an airtight container from the following day to retain their aroma and dampness. The peak of their season is April and May, although sometimes they can be found until June.

At Etxebarri they make the most of them by preparing them in two different ways: on the one hand, sliced raw if they go into scrambled eggs, or to top a cracker; and on the other, sautéed. Their aroma is most appreciated when they are raw, but when sautéed they have a more pronounced hint of woodiness. Although by subjecting St George's mushrooms to heat some of their aroma is lost, they become much juicier. Both raw and sautéed, they have aromatic characteristics reminiscent of truffles which is why they are so esteemed gastronomically.

ST GEORGE'S MUSHROOMS

SAUTÉED ST GEORGE'S MUSHROOMS

INGREDIENTS

— St George's mushrooms
— Olive oil

METHOD

— Choose the St George's mushrooms for their size: choose the smallest.

— Although they are quite clean mushrooms, clean them with a cloth without washing or wetting them.

— Spray the St George's mushrooms with olive oil and sauté them in a mesh pan for a minute at the most.

— Remove from the heat, season lightly with salt and serve.

SLICED ST GEORGE'S MUSHROOMS ON A CRACKER

When raw, the St George's mushrooms are served on a cracker. These unleavened wheat-flour crackers are served as an appetizer and spread with a cream of St George's mushrooms. To make the cream, cut up two St George's mushroom stems and confit them in olive oil over a low heat for two hours. Next, keep a few drops of oil aside, and process everything to a smooth paste and leave to cool.

The crispiness of the cracker is the perfect balance for the thick texture of the St George's mushrooms' cream. The St George's mushrooms are sliced over the cracker spread with the cream, seasoned with a pinch of salt and a few drops of the oil.

Hens roam free from the coop to the meadow outside Bittor's farmhouse. They are fed corn, barley, hay and grasses from the fields, in addition to eating seeds, insects and worms. They breathe clean air and lay one egg a day at the most. This results in eggs with extraordinary characteristics. Fabulous eggs with bright, orangey-yellow yolks that taste fresh and clean. Eggs that are so nutritious, healthy and flavoursome that they can be eaten raw.

At Etxebarri they are cooked, but only a little. They make scrambled eggs that are cooked at a very low temperature, without letting them set, with the aim of obtaining a creamy consistency. Freshness and creaminess are combined and enhanced by the aromas of truffles and St George's mushrooms. These scrambled eggs are served from October to June; with sliced white truffles from October to December, with black truffles from December to February, and with sliced and whole St George's mushrooms from April to June. A simple, gastronomic delicacy.

EGGS

SCRAMBLED EGGS WITH ST GEORGE'S MUSHROOMS OR BLACK OR WHITE TRUFFLE

INGREDIENTS

— 2 eggs (laid that day) from Bittor's farm

— 5 g white or black truffle (or 40 g St George's mushrooms)

— 50 ml olive oil

— Salt

METHOD

— Aromatise the olive oil with the trimmings from the St George's mushrooms and/or the truffle for 1 hour. Pour a few drops into a frying pan and place over a very low heat.

— Beat the yolks and the whites together in a bowl and season with salt.

— Before the frying pan gets hot, pour in the beaten eggs and stir constantly for 15 minutes or until the eggs have a creamy texture. As you cook, remove the frying pan from the heat if you see that the eggs are going to set. The secret is that they warm through and cook very gently, but do not set.

— Serve in a bowl and slice truffle and/or St George's mushrooms to taste over the yellow liquid.

Gastronomically considered to be the caviar of the vegetable world, the teardrop pea is not a variety in itself, but is a question of ripeness: they are picked just as the fruit of the plant forms and has the shape of a teardrop. This fruit contains proteins and sugars that, at this early stage, have not yet turned into starch. The result is a pea that bursts with flavour and freshness, a crunchy, creamy explosion as soon as you bite into it that then tastes of sweet grasses. It is so tender that it can be eaten raw.

Teardrop peas are eaten at Etxebarri for about six months of the year; the first batch comes from the Mediterranean and are picked in the middle of winter. This is followed by the season in the Basque Country that begins in April and extends to mid June. They are different varieties. Bittor prefers those grown in the Basque Country – either those from along the coast of Guipuzcoa or from his own vegetable garden in Axpe – because those from the Mediterranean have a slightly thicker skin and their texture is not quite as elegant.

They need a cool, damp environment to grow in, withstand the cold well but not like the heat or the wind. They are picked artisanally; by hand every day, and best done at dawn before the sun warms things up. There is not much to show for it; less than 100 grams per kilo picked. At Etxebarri they choose the smallest to serve as a dish and use the rest as an accompaniment, for instance for razor clams: the clam is placed on one shell and a line of sautéed peas are arranged on the other.

These pearls from his vegetable garden are served as a dish after being grilled in their pods, cooking en papillote, while the pods are infused with the aroma of the wood coals. The pods are blended to extract their juice that is slightly bitter and has a hint of smokiness.

TEARDROP PEAS IN THEIR JUICE

INGREDIENTS

— 100 g teardrop peas
— The juice from the pods of the peas
— Olive oil and salt

METHOD

— Lay the pods on the grill so that the peas cook inside them for 5 minutes on each side.

— Remove the pods from the fire, shell them and set the pods aside. Blend the pods to extract their juice, season lightly with salt and set aside.

— Choose the smallest peas, spray them with olive oil and sauté over lively wood coals for a few seconds in a mesh pan with tiny perforations. Remove when they have warmed through.

— Season with salt.

— Pour the pod juice over them when you plate the dish.

SAUTÉED BABY BROAD BEANS

The baby broad beans on Etxebarri's menu always come from Bittor's vegetable garden, the season coinciding with that of peas. As with peas, the most tender baby broad beans are the first to appear: they are the smallest, most elegant and have a characteristic bitter-sweet balance. The smallest are chosen to serve as a main course. They are sautéed in a mesh pan for a few seconds and, when they are about to be served, a little ham stock is added. Bigger baby broad beans are sautéed in the same way and served as an accompaniment for the sea cucumber recipe.

The recipe that began the revolution of Etxebarri's cuisine in 2000. The anchovy season on the Cantabrian coast spans from the start of April to June, although its peak is just before spawning at the beginning of the season (April-May). They have a pronounced flavour but at the same time they are the most elegant member of the oily fish family.

The perfect weight for grilling is 30 to 35 grams, although what is really important is how fresh they are. Those served at Etxebarri are from Ondárroa or Santoña and are fished at dawn on the same day they are eaten. They are delivered intact as they were not damaged when fished and their skin is smooth and shiny. Anchovies are very delicate creatures and deteriorate quickly after being taken from the sea. It is thus best to keep them in seawater and ice. At Etxebarri they are kept for no longer than 24 hours.

Two anchovy fillets are sandwiched together to make one double anchovy, the aim of which is to lightly smoke the flesh inside. The alternative, with single fillets, would be to grill them whole without removing the spine, but this makes it hard to grill them and the results are not the same.

On the grill, the aim is to achieve a very light cook that allows the flesh inside to remain rosy but not raw and, at the same time, juicy. It is also important that the heat penetrate gently so that they get hot all the way through. Their delicate texture, elegant mild flavour and the touch of smokiness make this recipe a sublime morsel.

ANCHOVIES

ANCHOVIES OVER WOOD COALS

INGREDIENTS

— 8 fresh anchovies
(for a serving of 4 double anchovies)

— 200 ml olive oil

— 1 small piece hot chilli pepper

— 200 ml Txakoli wine

— Guérande salt

— Rocket leaves

METHOD

— Use scissors to clean the anchovies: cut away part of their tails, cut off their heads and remove their innards. Butterfly the anchovies, remove the spines and pinbone the other bones. Quickly run under water and dry with a cloth.

— Place one anchovy on top of the other – flesh to flesh – so they form a single anchovy with only the skin showing. Tie them together at the tail.

— Spray the anchovies with olive oil to prevent them from drying. Place them in a flat, narrow grilling basket at a medium height and 15 centimetres from the wood coals. Grill over low embers between 1 and 2 minutes per side, depending on the thickness of the anchovies. Remove.

— Plate, sprinkle with a pinch of salt and add a few drops of hot oil with a hint of chilli and Txakoli.

— Serve with rocket dressed with olive oil.

This other delicacy of Basque gastronomy could not be missing at Etxebarri... hake kokotxas that bring together a silky texture, a pronounced taste of the sea, and the intensity of their gelatine. Although local recipes are mainly prepared with a pilpil sauce, or are battered, at Etxebarri they prefer not to mask them with anything so that all their subtleness can be appreciated. Because of their delicate texture, their treatment on the grill requires a clinical eye and great skill. When they come off the grill, they are dressed with a touch of green sauce.

For all of their properties to shine through, it is important that the hake be very fresh as it goes off very quickly. The best kokotxas are shiny and have a delicate, gelatinous texture. On the grill, the secret is for the fire to caress them gently, little more than two minutes each side over very low wood coals and at a medium height. They thus retain all their elegance, texture and delicacy while the flavour of the sea is also enhanced.

KOKOTXAS

HAKE KOKOTXAS OVER WOOD COALS

INGREDIENTS

— 3 x 70 g hake kokotxas

— 500 ml fish stock

— 1 clove garlic

— 3 parsley leaves

— 2 tbsp olive oil

— Salt

— Daikon radish or white asparagus (in season)

METHOD

— Cut the beards off the kokotxas and spray them with olive oil.

— Place them in a narrow grilling basket and grill for a maximum of two and a half minutes on each side over low wood coals and at a medium height.

— Season the kokotxas with a pinch of salt and remove from the grill.

— Finely chop the garlic and sweat it in olive oil without letting it brown. Add the gelatinous fish stock and stir to slightly thicken the green sauce. Add the chopped parsley.

— Spoon this traditional green sauce over the kokotxas and serve. They can also be served over daikon radish or white asparagus.

Bonito is one of the most delicate and subtle fish to be found in the Cantabrian Sea in the summer. Bittor prefers it to tuna not only due to its high fat content that gives better results on the grill, but because its flavour is also more pronounced. His choice cut is bonito belly whose flesh is fattier and whose flavour is more elegant, as well as having less muscle. But if this is not possible, he uses the fillets.

Either way, bonito needs an experienced hand at the grill because its delicate flesh and relatively fine thickness – barely two centimetres – allow no room for error. The aim is for it to be raw and juicy inside so that it remains nice and pink, but that it is warmed through. It is thus grilled over a small quantity of wood coals at a medium height, essentially just enough to sear both sides.

It is plated on a delicate emulsion of soy sauce, lemon juice, sunflower oil, olive oil and a thick stock made with bonito bones, and blended until thick, like an eggless mayonnaise. As their seasons coincide, it is served with marinated tomatoes from Bittor's vegetable garden. He also has a recipe for tuna belly or tuna loin that is almost exactly the same but requires more time on the grill, and the emulsion includes grated lemon zest.

BONITO BELLY

INGREDIENTS

— A bonito from the Cantabrian Sea
(for bellies weighing 100 - 120 g)

— A tomato from the vegetable garden

— 8 tbsp sunflower oil

— 4 tbsp olive oil

— 6 drops lemon juice

— 6 drops soy sauce

— 6 tbsp mineral water

— Salt

METHOD

— Gut the bonito, remove the head, cut off the fins and tail and remove the spine. Cut out the bellies and set them aside.

— To make the bonito stock, boil the bones in mineral water for 2 hours until it has reduced to the desired consistency. Set aside.

— Place the bellies on the main grill at a medium height and with low wood coals. Grill for 1 minute each side. Remove, season with salt and set aside.

— Pour the two oils, soy sauce, lemon juice and the bonito-bone stock into a bowl and emulsify to a mayonnaise-like consistency.

— Arrange the bonito bellies over the mayonnaise and serve with half a marinated tomato.

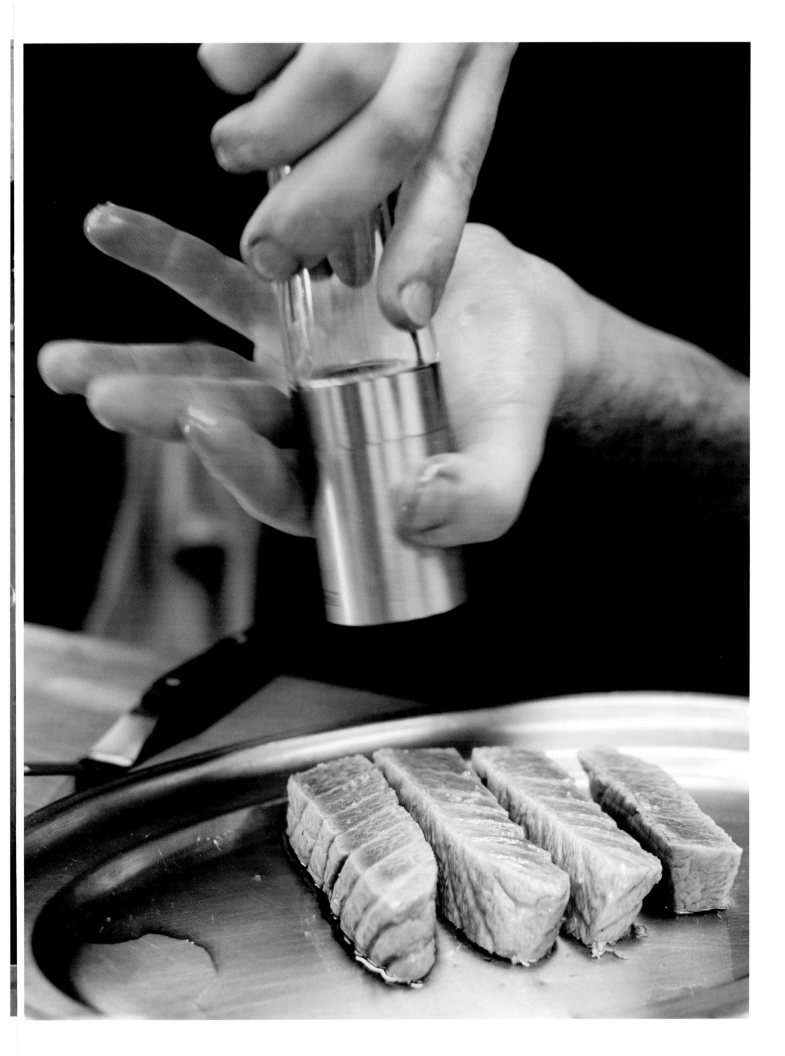

Maintaining the excellence of this traditional hallmark of Basque cuisine has become something of a challenge for Etxebarri. Over the years, and as a way of simplifying the process for curing salt cod, quality has waned. The challenge is to find salt cod that has been cured according to a natural process. Meticulous dehydration concentrates and enhances the delicious flavour of this fish.

Desalting it in cold water is a slower process, but it avoids the flesh from deteriorating, ensures it stays firm and keeps its attractive and uniform bright white colour. Extraordinary results arise from grilling salt cod: its flavour is cleaner and its texture – consistent, juicy and elegant – is enhanced. The hint of smokiness is the final flourish.

Grilling must be very gentle, and with few wood coals, so that the heat penetrates slowly and no gelatine is lost. As the flesh has no nerves, the salt cod flakes easily as soon as it is done, and so it is separated into large, juicy flakes. The salt cod served at Etxebarri is from Iceland and is line caught. They like large fish so that there is a lot of gelatine to prevent it drying out on the grill.

SALT COD

SALT COD WITH GRILLED BELL PEPPERS

INGREDIENTS

— 200 g thick salt cod loin (per serving)

— 2 roasted bell peppers

— 2 litres mineral water

— 1 tbsp extra virgin olive oil (per serving)

— 1 clove garlic

METHOD

— Hydrate the whole salt cod loins in a bowl of very cold water (about 2°C) for at least 4 days without changing the water. Refrigerate.

— Discard the water, pin bone the fish and remove all the bones.

— Desalt the fish for two days at 2°C, changing the water once a day but avoiding an increase in its temperature. Dry with a cloth.

— Cut into servings of about 200 g. Set aside.

Pilpil sauce

— Confit, at a low temperature, a whole garlic clove together with the scraps of the desalted salt cod in olive oil.

When it has cooked for 20 minutes, shake the pan gently in a circular motion to thicken the sauce. Keep it warm at about 50°C until needed; it is important that it stay at this temperature to remain thick.

Wood coals

— Arrange half-consumed wood coals under the grill.

— Spray the fish with olive oil to avoid it sticking to the grill. Place in a narrow grilling basket close to the fire, skin-side down.

— Grill over a low fire for 15 - 20 minutes skin-side down, and then for a further 5 - 10 minutes depending on the thickness. Remove when the flakes are well seared and separate easily.

— Plate, pour a little of the pilpil sauce over the top and serve with the roasted bell peppers.

An emblematic fish in Basque gastronomy, sea bream is a local species the numbers of which are dwindling although they are still fished in the waters of the Cantabrian Sea. They have been grilled at grill-houses in the Basque Country for as long as anyone can remember. The traditional recipe calls for the fish to be topped with garlic, chilli and vinegar fried in oil that, to be honest, doesn't really go with it.

Sea bream also features on the menu at Etxebarri, but they are served according to a revamped recipe that is based on the traditional one. For Bittor it is not just crucial that they come from the Cantabrian Sea, but that the ones served are caught from a boat from Bermeo that fishes in a specific fishing ground that guarantees large, fattier and more flavoursome, sea bream. Semi-fat fish, somewhere between oily fish and white fish, the levels of omega-3 fatty acids they contain depends on the time of year. In Bittor's opinion, they are at their peak between September and November.

Rounded fish with a lot of fat and thick skin, they are prefect for grilling. They can be placed very close to the wood coals before their skin starts burning; this means that they cook in their own juices and lose almost no liquid. And, when they are cut open, the flesh flakes perfectly and is very moist. A touch of freshness and acidity is added thanks to a less aggressive sauce than the traditional one; the vinegar is replaced by rhubarb water.

SEA BREAM

SEA BREAM OVER WOOD COALS

INGREDIENTS

— 1 sea bream weighing 1 kg

— 3 tbsp olive oil

— Rhubarb sticks

— Salt

METHOD

— Blend and strain the rhubarb to extract the juice. Set aside.

— Gut the sea bream, rinse under running water and dry with a cloth.

— Place the whole sea bream on the grill at a low height and very close to the fire. The wood coals should be very lively.

— Grill for 12 minutes on one side, then turn the fish over and grill for a further 8 minutes. Remove.

— Place the fish on a tray and cover it for 2 - 3 minutes with another tray so that it finishes cooking.

— Use a knife to cut it in half lengthways. Remove the spine and then pin bone the smaller bones. Season with salt.

— Fry the rhubarb juice and the juices on the tray released by the fish in the oil. Strain and emulsify. Pour a little over the fish.

WOODCOCK

METHOD

— Spray the woodcock with olive oil and roast, skin-side down, for six - seven minutes, depending on the size of the bird. Turn it over and roast for a further two minutes.

— Cut the head in half lengthwise and roast it over the wood coals for three minutes at the most, just enough to sear both sides. Season with salt when it comes off the grill and set it aside.

— As an accompaniment, serve sautéed chanterelles, hedgehog mushrooms or other wild, seasonal mushrooms, roasted beetroot and chestnuts, and beetroot shoots.

— Carve up the woodcock, separating the thighs from the breasts, and plate. Add the two halves of the head, the canapé of woodcock pâté and the accompaniment. Add a few brushstrokes of the woodcock sauce and serve.

BEEF CHOP
OVER WOOD COALS

INGREDIENTS

— 1 chop, 3 cm thick

— Fleur de sel de Guérande

— Vine roots and vine cuttings

METHOD

— Make lively wood coals with the vine roots and add the vine cuttings before placing the chop on the grill.

— Cut the chops to a thickness of 3 centimetres and place them on the grill at a height that is just above the flames.

— Season with salt on the raw, upper side. Grill for 10 minutes.

— Shake off the excess salt and turn the chop over. Grill for a further 5 minutes.

— Remove, serve, slice and plate with the corresponding accompaniment.

A benchmark dish of any grill-house worth its salt is roast kid or lamb. At Etxebarri kid is only served whole, and when ordered ahead of time. As a rule, they come from Yurre (in León), weigh between eight and ten kilos, and are exclusively milk fed. He alternates between suckling kid that are little more than 30 days old with slightly older ones that are about 45 days old and weigh ten kilos. The mothers eat only grass.

The diet of the mothers and their offspring is key for understanding the unique properties that kid meat has. The age of the creature means that the meat is tender and elegant and, because of the perfect amount of infiltrated stored fat, the meat is also very juicy and delicious. They are cooked traditionally in a wood-fired oven with water and salt.

Bittor uses the residual heat of one of his ovens, still hot from the lunchtime meal service of the previous day. They are roasted in an earthenware dish for two hours at a relatively low temperature as if slow cooked. In addition to absorbing the aroma of the wood coals, the kid is basted in a stock made of garlic, onion and white wine that is then emulsified with the juices and fat from the kid. It is served with Batavia lettuce on the side.

KID

OVEN ROASTED KID

INGREDIENTS

— 1 suckling kid weighing 10 kg

— 1.5 litres water

— 500 ml white wine

— 1 onion

— 4 cloves garlic

— 100 g lettuce (as an accompaniment)

— Salt

METHOD

— Cut the two kid halves in half at the height of the third rib. This will yield four pieces with a leg each. Sprinkle with salt.

— Put the quartered kid into an earthenware dish with mineral water in the bottom. Place in the residual oven at 200°C and roast for 105 minutes.

— Put another pan containing mineral water, white wine, garlic and onion into the same oven and allow it to simmer but not boil.

— After 105 minutes, remove the kid from the dish. Strain the liquid from the pan and combine with the kid's juices and fat in the bottom of the earthenware dish.

— Put the pieces of kid back in the dish and roast for a further 15 minutes on the other side, basting various times with the above-mentioned stock.

— Remove from the oven, plate and serve with the lettuce.

ACKNOWLEDGEMENTS

This book would never have seen the light of day if Bittor Arginzoniz had not dedicated countless hours to the authors to convey to them his culinary knowledge and philosophy, the particulars of his gastronomic creations and all the ups and downs of his past and his life. Needless to say, we offer him our sincerest thanks for his dedication and for having taken the time do so. Bittor's enthusiasm on our visits to Etxebarri was the impetus that made it possible for this book to come to fruition.

We extend our appreciation to Bittor's wife, Patricia Velar, always ready to help and always with a huge smile. Much of the time we required Bittor was taken over by her. Her contribution about life with Bittor and the history of Etxebarri were vital.

Our recognition also goes to the entire team at Etxebarri, especially because the dynamics of Etxebarri do not allow for much free time beyond the routines carried out every day.

In particular, we would like to thank Agustí Peris for his contribution in describing in detail the wines offered at the restaurant, for his accurate depiction of the reality at Etxebarri, and for going over the book's contents; to Eneko Díaz, for telling us about the restaurant's philosophical cornerstone, in addition to its pastry making; to Hector Gran, for his invaluable help in unravelling the secrets of the recipes; to Tetsuro Maeda, for shedding light on the virtues of each delicacy that he works with; and to Estela Izquierdo, for having an answer for everything. They all know, better than anyone, the way Bittor operates in the kitchen.

Our thanks also go to everyone who, in the world that revolves around Etxebarri, have contributed with their explanations and suggestions for improving the content of this book. Among them we would like to highlight Octavio, the suppliers of produce to Etxebarri, local woodcock hunters, elver fishermen, and gatherers of wild mushrooms.

We would particularly like to thank the contribution of Rafael García Santos. On the one hand for demystifying the conceptual foundations of Etxebarri's cuisine, as well as for sharing his decades-long relationship with Bittor for this book. On the other, for consolidating ideas and highlighting dishes, some no longer on the menu, that could not be left out. His approval has been essential.

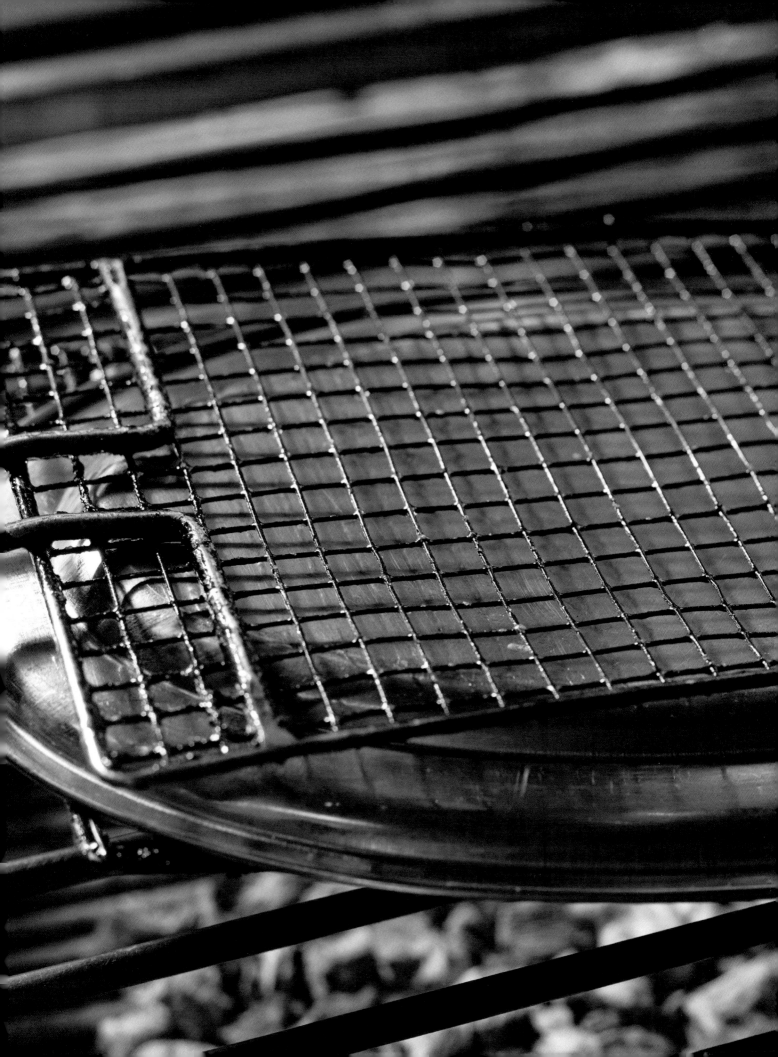

JUAN PABLO CARDENAL

JON SARABIA

MARIANO HERRERA

(Barcelona, 1968) is a journalist with a Master's Degree in International Relations, and with years of experience of travelling and in gastronomy. His articles have been published in well-known media, such as *El Mundo,* the magazine *GEO, La Clave* and *Siete Leguas,* among others. His passion for gastronomy, travelling and journalism gave rise to his writing the introductory texts for the book *Clorofilia* (2004) on Mugaritz; to exploring the four corners of China to write a travel guide about it (2005); and to being the co-author of *Elkano, A Culinary Landscape* (2016). He has also worked as a correspondent in China for a decade, writing articles for *The Economist, El Mundo, El País* and other international publications. Over the past years he has travelled to 40 countries to understand and explain how China is changing the world. Among others, he is the co-author of three books on the internationalization of China, published in Spain by the publishing house Crítica and translated into 11 languages.

(Bilbao, 1968) has a Degree in Business Administration and an MBA from IESE. He has worked as a banking executive (Banco Santander, CaixaBank) and has 20 years of experience in electronic channels and payment methods, consulting, and start-ups. A gastronomad by vocation, since 2014 he has written about wine and gastronomy, collaborating with Michelin-starred chefs and restaurateurs who regularly appear on the *50 Best list. Xemei, Cocina Venexiana* (2016) was the first book he wrote and the first book published by Planeta Gastro, the trade name of Grupo Planeta which he advises as director of the collection. He is a member of the Acadèmia Catalana de Gastronomia i Nutrició.

(Buenos Aires, 1970) trained at the Escuela Argentina de Fotografía and from the age of twenty-two has worked as a freelance photographer. Now settled in Barcelona, he regularly contributes to publications such as *Monocle, Esquire* and *El País Semanal* with his photographs and portraits. As an advertising photographer he has taken part in numerous Spanish and international campaigns, among which is the outstanding 'Cerca', for Banc Sabadell, with Rafa Nadal as its protagonist. His photographs for *Xemei, Cocina Venexiana* (2016) were chosen by Food Photo Festival in Vejle (Denmark), for which he provided the official 2015 image. He has also taught at the Escuela de Diseño Elisava in Barcelona.

TODAY, WE HAVE...

BUTTER

FRESH CHEESE

CHORIZO

CROQUETTE

TOMATO

PUMPKIN

SALMON

CRAB

VELVET CRAB

GOOSE-NECK BARNACLES

CLAMS, COCKLES AND
WARTY VENUS CLAMS

VARIEGATED SCALLOPS

MUSSELS

OYSTERS

CAVIAR

LANGOUSTINES / LOBSTER

PRAWNS FROM PALAMÓS

SEA CUCUMBER

ELVERS

BABY OCTOPUSES

YOUNG SQUID

PEPPER

WILD MUSHROOMS
AND AUBERGINES

MARCH MUSHROOMS

ST GEORGE'S MUSHROOMS

EGGS

ARTICHOKES

TEARDROP PEAS

ANCHOVIES

KOKOTXAS

RED MULLET

BONITO

GROUPER

SALT COD

SEA BREAM

WOODCOCK

BEEF CHOP

KID

DESSERTS

MILK ICE CREAM

CHEESE CRÈME CARAMEL

JUNKET

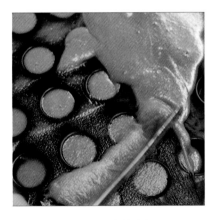

MADELEINES

COCOA SHOT

CREDITS

This English language edition first published in 2018 by
Grub Street
4 Rainham Close
London SW11 6SS

Reprinted 2018

Email: food@grubstreet.co.uk
Twitter: @grub_street
Facebook: Grub Street Publishing
Web: www.grubstreet.co.uk

Copyright this English language edition © Grub Street 2018

First published in Spanish by Editorial Planeta, S. A., 2017
Text copyright © Bittor Arginzoniz, Juan Pablo Cardenal
   and Jon Sarabia
Photography copyright ©Mariano Herrera
Photography copyright © p. 331, James G. Y. (J. P. Cardenal)
   and Yaiza P. Colino (J. Sarabia)
Project Editor: Jon Sarabia
Design: Atlas
Cover design: Daniele Roa

A CIP record for this title is available from the British Library

ISBN: 9781911621218

All rights reserved. No part of this book may be reproduced
or transmitted in any form or by any means, electronic
or mechanical, including photocopying, recording or any
information storage and retrieval system, without permission
in writing from the publisher.

Printed and bound in Slovenia

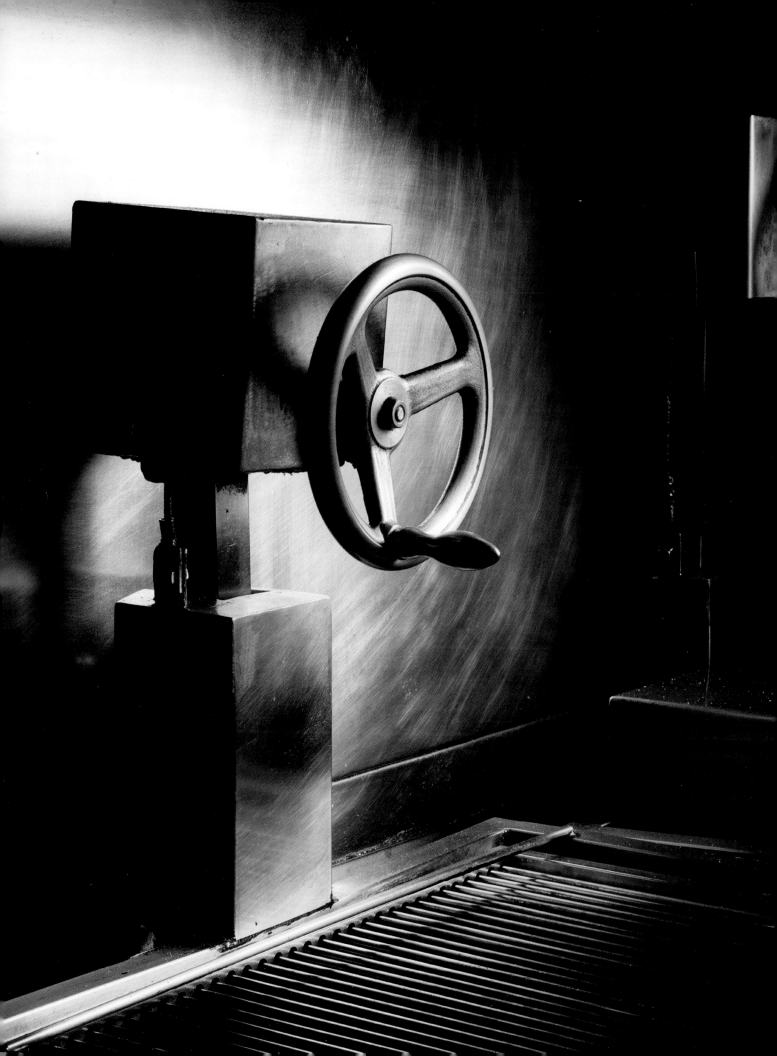